D0261930

69 For 1

By the same author

The Dog it Was That Died
All Except the Bastard
The Sanity Inspector
Golfing for Cats
The Collected Bulletins of Idi Amin
The Further Bulletins of Idi Amin
The Lady From Stalingrad Mansions
The Peanut Papers
The Rhinestone as Big as the Ritz
Tissues for Men
The Best of Alan Coren
The Cricklewood Diet
Bumf
Present Laughter (Editor)
Something for the Weekend?
Bin Ends
Seems Like Old Times
More Like Old Times
A Year in Cricklewood
Toujours Cricklewood
Alan Coren's Sunday Best
Animal Passions (Editor)
A Bit on the Side
The Cricklewood Dome
The Alan Coren Omnibus
Waiting for Jeffrey

For children

Buffalo Arthur
The Lone Arthur
Arthur the Kid
Railroad Arthur
Klondike Arthur
Arthur's Last Stand
Arthur and the Great Detective
Arthur and the Bellybutton Diamond
Arthur v the Rest
Arthur and the Purple Panic

69 For 1

ALAN COREN

First published in Great Britain in 2007 by JR Books, 10 Greenland Street, London NW1 0ND www.jrbooks.com

A catalogue record for this book is available from the British Library.

ISBN 978-1-906217-36-5

1 3 5 7 9 10 8 6 4 2

Printed by MPG Books, Bodmin, Cornwall

Contents

69 For 1

YOU have just picked this up in your local bookshop, to have a bit of a flip, have a bit of a dip, possibly have a root around in your wallet – if I can give you some idea of what *69 For* 1 means. Tricky. If I were Humpty Dumpty I might declare that it means just what I choose it to mean, and since I have, as you will shortly hear, much in common with Humpty Dumpty, I suppose I could leave it at that; but I shan't, because you might irritably snap the book shut and look for something by a less arrogant hack.

69 For 1 means two things – neither of them sexual, since you ask, otherwise it would be called 69 For 2 – and the first thing it means is that 69 pieces constitute 1 book. The second thing is that the author of these pieces has just become 69. Nothing to celebrate there, you say, no kind of milestone, but it is for me, because I nearly didn't become it. Last year, I was very nearly 68 all out. That is the much I have in common with Humpty Dumpty; the one thing we do not, fortunately, have in common, is that all the king's horses and all the king's men were able to put me together again. Or, rather, all the king's physicians, surgeons, anaesthetists, radiographers, nurses, etc, since had it been left to his horses, I should unquestionably have been done for.

What nearly did that, mind, nobody knows for sure; but on a hot summer's night last year, spotting me in the French moonlight, something bit me as I snored: could have been a gnat, could have been a scorpion, could have been a werewolf, it left no note, merely a breach into which a billion opportunist streptococci plunged and set up a colony called Septicaemia. It is an inclement little country, where your flesh falls off, thanks to the national sport: sassy newspapers call it necrotising fasciitis, the red-tops prefer flesh-eating disease, but however you slice it, slicing it is what has to be done, and within a couple of hours that is what the terrific surgeons of Nice's Hôpital Saint-Roche were doing.

They put my conked-out organs on a lot of machines to do it, too, and kept me on them for ages, seriously threatening the French National Grid: a thousand kilometres away, Parisian diners would glance up from their *soupe de poisson* and wonder why the lights were flickering.

I stayed in the coma for a month, and while, when I eventually emerged, it was a considerable relief to my dearest – who had become even more my nearest by putting their lives on hold in order to be there for mine – it was something of a disappointment, too. For by Hollywood tradition, when a month-long sleeper emerges from his coma, he either cries 'Hallo trees! Hallo sky!' to his surrounding loved ones, or else explains to them that he had the near-death experience of floating through a long tunnel at the end of which (in my case, at least) James Thurber and Bernard Levin were waiting with a dry martini to welcome him aboard and direct him to the wingmakers.

According, however, to Mrs Coren and my children, my first words were 'Get me a hand-grenade!', because, they discovered as I gabbled on, I had got it into my comatose head that I was in occupied France, and the Boche were at the gate, drawn thither by collaborators who had spotted the shortwave radio in the cardboard suitcase under my bed.

Fortunately, my clapped-out mind was eventually set at rest, and returned with my repairing body to England, where it soon became 69. So I am the one for which 69 is. I did think of calling the book *69 Not Out,* but then I had this feeling that I'd already tempted providence enough.

Beyond Our Ken

IN the high and far off times, Best Beloved, before the good Lord smiled upon him and made him my gracious Mayor, Ken Livingstone and I both lived in Cricklewood, a stone's throw from one another; though this distance, despite the occasional temptation, was never actually verified. Since then we have both moved closer to the epicentre of the fiefdom he has made all his own, but, because you may take the boy out of Cricklewood but not Cricklewood out of the boy, our paths, I find, have crossed again. Yokels both, each had his dream of the metropolis; but, heartbreakingly, they have turned out to be very different dreams. I never guessed: though I have run into him a fair few times since those idyllic peripolitan days, mostly when we were engaged upon daft broadcast parlour games concerned with bluff, deceit and guesswork – at all of which Ken unsurprisingly proved to be brilliantly adept – we never talked about these dreams of ours. But it is time to talk of them now, before it is too late for either of us.

The Mayor, I learn from an exhibition at his shiny new City Hall, has a vision of transfiguring the Marylebone

Road: he wishes it not only to become London's Champs-Elysées but to be connected via Regent's Park to Primrose Hill, a mile or so to its north, by a further broad boulevard, and by a yet further broader one, to Bankside in the south. Ken's field of dreams is the Fields of Heaven. Silly arse.

Do I hear you cry that this slur is as gratuitously offensive as it is utterly baffling, given that the very place where I now hang my Cricklewood hat-collection lies bang in the middle of Regent's Park, between Primrose Hill and the Marylebone Road, exactly equidistant from each and thus the very nub of what will be the wondrous Champs Livingstone? How can I not relish the notion of, any day now, springing down my front steps on a fine summer morning, twirling my malacca cane, to join the elegant throng of coutured boulevardiers strolling the broad avenues beneath the sighing shade-trees, pausing only to tip my panama and exchange charming compliments and scintillating ripostes before popping in to take a *filtre et fine* at any one of a hundred fashionable pavement cafes, every one of them packed to the geranium gunwales with the artists and writers and singers and actors who have flocked here from all over the world? Oh, look, isn't that Pablo Hirst doodling dots on a menu that will make his waiter rich, even as, beside him, F. Scott Amis explains to Salman Hemingway that the rich are different from you and me, while his wife Zelda pirouettes naked atop a passing taxi ('You'll never guess who I had on the roof of the cab last week'), and blow me down if that isn't Gertrude Rowling telling Enrico Manilow that a nose is a nose is a nose, to the delighted doeskin-clad clapping of some 83 of the ravishing catwalk soubrettes who have recently appeared in *The Vagina Monologues* and are therefore here this morning to pose for the magic brush of Rolf de Toulouse-Lautrec.

Oh, get off! 'This is London', as Britain used to Morse to France in the days when the Champs-Elysées teemed shoulder-to-shoulder with marching Nazis, delighted to have found a street roomy enough to do their thing in; because the Champs-Elysées, may I remind Ken, is six times wider than the Marylebone Road. Indeed, it has more than once occurred to me that Hitler may well have abandoned his 1940 invasion plans for no better reason than that London's main thoroughfares were so narrow: had they all parachuted onto Hampstead Heath, as was mooted, it is more than likely that the German Army would have jackbooted into gridlock halfway down Finchley Road, where they would have been picked off like fish in a barrel.

So then, where do I begin, if I am to list the doubts about the end to which Ken's vision might bring us? With the kinds of catering establishments bound to be clogging the skimpy pavements bordering the already sclerotic tarmac, al fresco Burger Kings and Pizza Huts, KFCs and Kebaboramas, Starbucks and Bella Pastas and Slug & Lettuces? With their rowdy 24/7 lagered clientele, undraped beer-bellies lobstering in the sun, gobbing at the stationary traffic four feet from the table they are waiting to throw at the Man U chara-convoy which cellphoned pickets have told them is just coming off the M1? With the million class-actions brought by fast-food, booze and fag addicts, not to mention as many diesel-wheezers, hoping to empty the coffers of the man who, at a stroke, doubled their exposure to all of the above? Maybe that alone will stay his hand.

But it may not help. I hear there is an alternative plan to demolish the flood-barriers and let the Thames fill London. Why not? It worked for Venice.

Low Country

DURING a recent fireside chat, my dear chum Libby Purves made my spirits soar. Not, of course, for the first time; but never yet so aptly, since what she was addressing was what makes spirits plummet, and what to do about it. Despite the dispiriting news that 31 million prescriptions were last year scrawled for them, she was tooting the horn for antidepressants. Purves says Prozac's all right.

Now, I am not normally depressed. But as shades of the pension house begin to close upon the growing boy, there are moments when I find myself staring into drizzle which isn't actually there; and yesterday, willy-nilly, it started coming down cats and dogs, because, before I ran into Libby, I had just read the Essex University report claiming that a better cure for depression than pills was a walk in the country.

My boots filled with sunken heart: for if I ever get depressed enough to need a walk in the country, I shall come home twice as depressed as I was before. I have done walks in the country when I was not at all depressed, and though I would set off like Julie Andrews, I would come back like Edvard Munch. That is because nothing makes me glummer than not knowing anything, and nothing has anything I know less about than the country. The country is another country: they do things differently there.

Oh, look, a tree. A larch? A beech? A birch? To me, they are as indistinguishable as the Wodehouse butlers they might as well be. The only tree I can identify is a horse-chestnut, but only if it has conkers on. What bird was that? I have a field guide, let me look it up, did it have a red speck on its beak, a green flash on its tail? It shot by like a feathered bullet, so who can say? Was it 'plink-plink-plink' it trilled, or 'tok-tok-tok'? Have I just seen an auk?

Aha, a field! Meadow? Dale? Wold? Let me negotiate this stile for a better view, if only of the nearest chiropractor. See, there are wild flowers! Of some kind. Possibly a variety of wort. I have heard there are a lot. Shall I eat this berry? Is it a sloe, a hip, or a thing for which the only antidote has immediately to be flown in from Sarawak? And might this be a farmer's dog bounding towards me? When will it stop bounding? Where is the bloody farmer? Is the dog protecting a cow which has appeared between me and the stile, or is it drawing a bull's attention to a vulnerable limper? Let me pop through this hedge which, goodness me, has so prettily grown over a barbed wire fence; was it as much fun as this on the Somme?

But see, with 34 bounds I am free! I never liked that jacket anyhow, it stood between me and the bracing chill of sleet, and hopping furrows on one boot must do wonders for something, because that is what the country is all about. It is very possibly what inspired Eli Lilly to hobble home to his snug, dungfree, gnatless, urban laboratory one soaking night and invent Prozac.

Shell Game

HERE is a little riddle to keep you occupied until you're ready for the next paragraph: what's twice the price of caviar and travels at half a mile an hour?

Well, clever old you. Fancy knowing that. I didn't know it until just a few minutes back, because I am more old than clever, and thus all I know is that 53 years ago what travelled at half a mile an hour was only twice the price of wine gums. And I know this because that is exactly what I paid for it.

Shall we extrapolate some quite remarkable facts from this? Such as the fact that what I once paid a shilling for is in all probability still travelling, and in covering, where's that calculator, 239,000 miles, not only has it not worn out, it has made itself worth 22,000 times more than I shelled out for it. Shelled out, for those who fell at the riddle hurdle, not coughed up: I'm helping you as much as I can. You'll agree that that is one hell of an investment; at least, it would be if I knew where it was, but since it has gone around the world ten times since I last saw it, it could be anywhere. Sorry, I don't want to mislead you, nor to exaggerate – those two authentic statistics having already made a mockery of exaggeration – it couldn't be anywhere in the world, it could only be anywhere in Britain, and mainland Britain, at that. Because not only is it worth its weight in gold, it has the same buoyancy. It cannot handle sea. It sinks.

Now, on the outside chance that there may be a handful among those beaten by both the riddle and the subsequent big fat clue who have not yet, miraculously, lost patience with all of this and turned gratefully to Jilly Cooper, where readers do not get mucked about, come with me, those few minutes back, to Palmer's Pet Stores in Camden Town. I am standing outside it, because I have not come to Camden Town to buy a pet, I have come to buy a leg of lamb, and you cannot buy a leg of lamb in Palmer's – unless, I suppose, it is still attached, this is the world's greatest pet shop, it does everything – but, as I stand outside, an idea sidles into my head. It sidles there because I have stood here before, in the sweet lang syne of 1950, with a birthday shilling hot in my hand. Thus I did not, on this latter morning, pass on to the butcher's, I went into Palmer's.

'Do you,' I said, 'still sell tortoises?'

'Upstairs,' said the assistant. 'Turn right at the spiders.'

So I did. It wasn't easy: what he should have said was turn green at the spiders, because these were no ordinary spiders, these were giant crabs in ginger wigs, these were octopod kittens, but I edged by somehow, and there, in the room next door, in a titchy glass box, was something about an inch across. I put my reading glasses on. It was a tortoise, all right. It may have looked up at me. It was hard to tell; it could have been lifting its tail.

'Do you have anything larger?' I said. 'I might lose this little chap in the garden; he could be trodden on, he could be swallowed by a cat, he could be lifted by a crow. He might even by dragged away by ants.'

'She,' said the salesman (what eyesight!), 'isn't ready for the garden yet. You'd have to keep her in a vivarium until she was big enough to look after herself. It'd take a good few years, mind.'

'How much is she?' I asked.

'£300,' he replied.

You all know what I said next, after I had steadied myself on the counter and stared at him for a bit, because you have been there with me. 'The last tortoise I bought here,' I said, 'cost me a shilling.'

'How much was a shilling?' he said.

'Put it this way,' I said, 'for £300 in 1950, I could've bought six thousand tortoises. I'd be rich man now. I'd be worth two million quid. Make that five million: mine was as big as a brick. You could mistake this one for a snail.'

'Yours would have been imported,' said the assistant. 'They used to come in by the truckload, but there's laws now. This one was born and bred here. She's English.'

'I'll keep my voice down, then,' I said. 'I'd hate to upset her. Don't you think £300 is a bit steep for a tortoise the size of my watch?'

'She's cheaper than a pedigree dog,' he said. 'Buy a puppy for £300, it'll live 15 years. If you're lucky. That's £20 a year. This tortoise could live to 100. So each year costs only three quid.' He grinned. 'Also, on your reckoning, she could be worth a couple of billion by then.'

'You're not wrong,' I said, 'but there's just one snag.'

'Which is?'

'I'd have to live to 165,' I said, and I went out, and round the corner, and got change out of a tenner. You know where you are, with a leg of lamb.

All Quiet On The Charity Front

As you know, many supermarkets, local authorities, and even some branches of the Royal British Legion have stopped issuing pins with poppies this year, lest people not merely prick their fingers, but also claim compensation for wounds. Understandable, given these poignant memoirs of one veteran Poppy Day survivor, which I make no excuse, on this special day, for quoting:

There was three of us up there that morning, in the thick of it as per usual, me, Chalky White and Nobby Clarke. The rain was coming down stair-rods, the wind went through you like a wossname, knife, but the mud was the worst. Slip off the pavement and you was done for; the lads do not call white vans whizz-bangs for nothing, you never hear the one that gets you.

Anyway, we was all keeping our heads down, because there was poppy-sellers all over; they'd moved up in the night and now they was in position everywhere, but you couldn't hardly see most of them, they are crafty buggers, you got to give them that, you see an empty doorway, you reckon you're all right, and suddenly they spring out from nowhere, they are on you before you know it. That is how they got Chalky that morning: we was creeping along, staying close to the wall, we was all but at the pub, we could hear blokes getting 'em in, we could smell roll-ups, and then Chalky only goes and sticks his head over the top for a shufti, and suddenly me and Nobby hears that terrible rattle what is like nothing else on God's earth, and poor old

Chalky finds hisself looking down the wrong end of a collecting tin.

Course, me and Nobby stood up as well, it is one for all and all for one in our mob, and we marched out, heads up, bags of swank, and Chalky shouts: 'Wiffel ist es, Kamerad?' because he has always been a bit of a wag, he does not let things get him down, nil carborundum, and this woman takes his ten pee and she gives him one of them looks they have, they are not like us, never will be, and hands him a poppy and a pin, and he says, 'Aren't you going to pin it on for me, Fraulein?' and she says, 'You want a lot for ten pee,' so I say, 'Leave it out, Chalky, it is not worth it, I'll do it, come here,' and I hold the poppy against his lapel and I take the pin and Chalky says, 'Is this the Big Push they're always going on about?' and I laugh so much that the pin goes and sticks right in my finger.

Blood gushed out. I must have lost very nearly a blob. 'Stone me!' yells Nobby. 'That is a Blighty one and no mistake. You will have to go straight home and put an Elastoplast on it.' Chalky looks at the woman. 'This is the bravest man I know,' he says. 'He has got his knees brown, he has done his bit, but that does not mean he likes the taste of cold steel up him. Look at that finger of his. It will not grow old as we that are left grow old. It may very well end up with a little scar on it. It might even turn sceptic and drop off into some corner of a foreign wossname, he will never be able to find it. So gimme my ten pee back.'

At this, despite the agony and spots before the eyes, I wade in, too; do not call me a hero, mind, I was just doing what any man would do in the circumstances, you would do the same. 'As soon I get this finger seen to,' I inform her, 'I shall be using it to dial my brief!'

At this, she lets out a shriek, chucks the ten pee at us, and runs off. Typical or what? They do not have no bottle, poppy-sellers: oh, sure, they may look hot as mustard quartered safe behind their lines, parading up and down outside Harrods in their spotless Barbours and their cashmere twinsets, with the sun winking off of their diamand brooches, and all smelling of Channel 4, but it is a very different matter up the sharp end in Lewisham, there is more to poppying out here than bull and bloody blanco. Me and Nobby and Chalky watched her skedaddle, and we gave a bit of a cheer, and then Nobby took my feet and Chalky held me under the arms, and they carried me past a number of material witnesses into the Rat and Cockle, and Chalky went off to get them in, and Nobby lit a fag and put it in my mouth, and he said: 'Could have been worse, mate – suppose it had been her what had stuck it in Chalky? He would have been pushing up daisies by now.'

'She might have got both of you,' I said. Nobby shook his head. 'No chance. One of 'em tried once, caught me off guard, took a quid off of me and before I could stop her she had shoved a pin straight through my lapel. It might have done me serious mischief if it wasn't for the Bible I always keep in my breast-pocket. I found it in a hotel bedroom, you know.'

'Bloody lucky,' I said. 'It could so easily have been a towel.'

'Or a rubber shower-mat,' said Chalky, setting down the drinks.

'A man needs a bit of luck,' said Nobby, 'out here.'

See How They Run

It is a sobering thought – unless you tied on something so celebratory last night as to leave you squinting at this through one throbbing eye, in which case a raw egg in a quart of espresso would doubtless serve you better – that if Athens had been only a mile down the road as Pheidippides flew, you would have had nothing to celebrate, since Sir Ranulph Fiennes would have spent last week at home with his feet up, watching *Countdown* .He would not have been blistering those feet around the world, 26 miles and 385 yards at a time, in his madcap triumph of running a marathon on seven continents in seven days, because there would be no such thing as a marathon.

He is not the first person to be have been driven nuts by this poxy event: click on almost any channel at almost any time, and chances are you will see thousands gasping through Wigan or Amarillo or Ulan Bator, variously got up as Napoleon and King Kong and Donald Duck and sucking on Volvic teats, while night begins to fold them in soft wings, because many hours have passed since the winner breasted the tape and went off to sign fat contracts with Lucozade or Nike. No other athletics' contest attracts losers the way the marathon does: you will not see spindly men in George Bush masks and sequinned tutus queuing up to put the shot a tad further, with any luck, than their toe, nor diving-suited crackpots trying to pole-vault a bar challengingly set at three inches, nor pantomime horses containing two fat grannies lumbering asymmetrically towards a sandpit for what might just become the sextuple jump, if they ever get there alive. But convene a marathon, and anything goes; for the most part slowly, and too often facetiously.

Yet worse – because, when it is merely a telly being plodded across, we idling pizza-gobblers may staunch our couchbound guilt with a swift athletic jab on the remote – is that real-life full-size marathoners are all out there, all the time, obsessively training in the pitiably inextinguishable hope of, someday, coming in 963rd. You cannot, these days, take an unobstructed stroll down any street: be sure that something wet and wheezing will either be clumping towards you, forcing you aside (since it cannot deviate, for fear of knocking a precious nano-second off its eight-hour target), or, far horribler, invisibly panting up behind you on thumping feet, forcing you to wonder whether there's enough time to swallow your mobile and disappear your wallet between your trembling buttocks before the lead pipe falls.

Even if you're not on the pavement but sealed in your car, they are still unavoidable. Try to ignore them as they suddenly spring out from the kerb – because jogging on the spot at the red light might ruin their chance of getting back to the office clock in the qualifying time required for them to represent Morgan Sachs against Goldman Waterhouse in this year's Pork Belly Futures Marathon – and they will, at the very least, scream and shout and throw their half-eaten bananas at you, or, at the very most, fly somersaulting off your nearside wing and make a nasty dent in your no-claims bonus.

Nor are the odds against their running into you any longer if you stay indoors. You will be on the easeful point, perhaps, of uncorking a little light lunch, when the doorbell rings, dragging you from your ottoman to a front step on which a man in a steaming vest is hopping up and down, either rattling a tin or waving a clipboard and pen. If it is the one with a tin, he is running from Potters Bar to Croydon and wants his money now, if it is the one with a clipboard and pen, he will be running from Croydon to Potters Bar next Tuesday and wants to come back for his money after he's done it.

Yes, yes, I know, don't go snatching up your own pen, I do realise it isn't his money, it will all go to charity, but that's not the point. The point is that though marathons may be useful in raising funds, they are useless in themselves: Pheidippides was not just the first man with a good reason to run 26 miles and 385 yards, he was also the last. All the modern marathon does is encourage its hapless fans to pant themselves purple for hundreds of hours, because – let us not beat about the bush, which, indeed, many of them are dressed as – they enjoy it. By that token, I could stand in Oxford Street buttonholing shoppers with the news that I had just watched *Friends* in aid of the RSPCA, see this tin, please dig deep, or go (slowly) round with a clipboard and pen begging the doorstepped to support my attempt, next Tuesday, to eat a kilo of caviar for Oxfam – which I could do without getting in anyone's way or frightening the horses. Moreover, lest you think me less than selfless, I'd be perfectly happy to do it in a luminous thong and antlers.

Suffer Little Children

YES, of course today's farrago is going to be about children no longer falling out of trees. You know the way I work: within seconds of my clocking what the NHS sees as this wonderful news in Monday's papers, my trouser leg was rolled up and my finger running along my shin and down the arches of the years. To end up, as you see, on my keyboard.

It's a knobbly johnny, this shin, and distinguishes me from Proust in that I do not need to dunk it in my tea to summon up the past: touching it, I touch again the just-plucked conkers in my plummeting grasp as Cecil Road leaps up to break me, I smell the sheets of Southgate Hospital, I hear the crackle of the nursing starch, I feel the itch beneath the plaster tube, all that.

I can call up this nostalgic stuff from almost anywhere: my whole body is a monument to risky youth. See that scar over my eye? A cocoa wound. What you did was, you emptied the cocoa tin, punched a pin-prick in its bottom, put your thumb over the hole to prevent the coal-gas you'd filled the tin with from escaping, ran into the garden, put the tin on the wall, backed off, then threw a flaming ball of paper at it, so that it could fragment like a hand-grenade and slice off enough of your face to merit six stitches.

See this scar in my left palm? Mobile phone wound. In 1950? All right, cocoa. What you did was, you emptied the cocoa tin, punched a pin-prick in its bottom, and threaded fifty yards of string through to attach to David Bunyan's cocoa tin at Number 16, making, once you'd leant out of your two windows and stretched the string taut, two mobile phones. The tauter you stretched it, the better the reception. Until one mobile phone flew from your hand and went through your father's greenhouse roof, enabling you to retrieve it for hardly more than six stitches.

The scar in my right palm? How you punched holes in cocoa tins was with a jack-knife: to do it, you unfolded the spike for taking stones out of horses' hooves, which, quite often, folded itself back as you punched. Just think what livid boyhood mementoes I might have earned, had I ever come across a limping horse!

That little white dent in my thigh, since you ask, was caused by an air-gun pellet. It was aimed by John Paige at a squirrel in the allotments so that we could go to the town hall and get a shilling for its tail, thanks to food-rationing: people grew things which got eaten by squirrels, so you shot them and cut their tails off to prove it to the council. In principle.

The big white dent in my thumb arrived soon after I told my father I was big enough to swing the Riley's starting-handle without hurting myself.

By the way, the NHS report which noted that tree-falling had gone down by 36 per cent in the last seven years also noted that RSI from computer games had gone up by 36 per cent. It's something, I suppose, but hardly the stuff of memory.

Not Found, Wanting

A FAIR few years back, in Finchley Road underground station, I found myself standing on a platform. Not much of an opening sentence, is it? Not exactly a gripper, not likely to bring you to the edge of your seat, not the sort of opening sentence calculated to have the entire population, infant and adult, queuing outside Waterstone's with their hearts pitter-pattering as Big Ben clunks towards midnight, frantic to know where that sentence might lead.

But wait. This was no ordinary platform I was standing on. It was itself standing on a platform. I was standing on a platform on a platform. With a penny in my hand. Which, this being a fair few years back, was a big penny. It was going into a slot. And if yet further evidence were needed that this was a fair few years back, after it had gone into the slot a deep voice said: 'You are ten stone seven pounds.' It wouldn't say it now: glance at the snapshot on this book's jacket and you will see that the chins alone weigh close to that. But I shall never be able to find out what the big deep voice would say now, because there are no speak-your-weight machines any more.

I speak this with the weight of authority. The authority is the Avery Historical Weighing Museum (oh yes there is), and even they haven't got one. I rang them this morning after I had rung every scales' manufacturer in the *Yellow Pages* to try to buy one, and the museum ruefully reported that they nearly got their hands on one a year or so ago, but the auctioneer knocked it down to an American for umpteen thousand pounds. Americans, it seems, collect them. It is hard to understand why: given the weight of most Americans, you would think they'd prefer to keep quiet about it, rather than have a thing on their premises shouting 'You are 290 pounds and you are killing both of us!', especially if the bathroom window is open.

Why did I do all this telephoning? Because I have a friend of a certain age who has a birthday coming up, and who has been advised of the uncertainty of age and the risk of future birthdays not coming up unless he loses weight, and I thought it might be both the action of a friend and a bit of fun to buy him a machine which would verbally encourage slimming. That and the fact that there's not much else to buy old fat blokes. But I have been thwarted, and since I do not take lightly to thwarting, I have also been thinking: why, when they were everywhere when I was young, are there no speak-your-weight machines any more?

Is it because we, running the Americans close – or, rather, lumbering them close – are so much fatter than we used to be? Obesity is all about us these days, and since it is all about everything from social and sexual undesirability to premature clogpopping, it may well be that the market for the public announcement of weight has vanished: not only do we not want the rest of the mob in Finchley Road tube station to turn, goggle, and snigger, we fear that the news might reach doctors who will refuse to treat us, insurance companies who will refuse to indemnify us, airlines who will refuse to carry us, employers who will refuse to promote us, and women who will twig that we are holding our stomachs in. Or, if not that, might it be the era's fashionable correctnesses that have dissuaded manufacturers from staying in business? Voices carry baggage: the old machines talked posh, but these days they would have to talk not merely common, too, but regional and ethnic; they would have to display buttons inviting the weighee to choose Estuary or Scouse or Welsh or Gujurat or Xhosa or Urdu or Yiddish, lest the machine find itself trolleyed off by the Council for Racial Equality and summoned to argue its defence before the European Court in Luxembourg, probably in both French and Walloon, or, at the very least, Esperanto.

Then there's violence. Or, rather, now there's violence: then, railway platforms were safe places, the worst you could get in your eye was a piece of soot which Trevor Howard would effortlessly remove, before buying you a convalescent rock cake. Now what you get in your eye is a fist. If a thug, illiterate, drunk, drugged, all three, poked his coin in something, and, instead of passing him a Mars bar, it told him, in Swahili, that he was 14 stone, he would almost certainly thump it, breaking a knuckle, and in consequence successfully suing the scales, manufacturer, Mars, Connex South Eastern, the Health & Safety Executive, and the headmaster who began all this by giving him a detention for bringing his Kalashnikov to school.

So there we are. Not much of an opening sentence, it wasn't Harry Potter & the Weighing Machine, but at least it didn't take 766 pages, and it may have struck a chord. If only with readers who were ten stone seven, once.

Gloss Finish

OH, comfort and joy! And could there be timelier tidings of them? My first yuletide presents are not merely arriving, they are arriving by the bagload! Every morning, at the thrilling clunk of the letter-box, I fly downstairs, and, yes, look, there are another three shimmering on the mat, each even more mouth-wateringly sumptuous than yesterday's. Christmas gift catalogues.

Whether you're a stressed executive, a busy housewife, a boisterous child, a hard-to-please teenager, or just a lively pensioner at a loose end, you can derive both endless pleasure and tension-relieving fun with these fabulously opulent artefacts in which traditional craftsmanship and cutting-edge innovation combine to produce a truly premier product. Each must-have catalogue comes in its own fully transparent envelope, expertly fashioned out of non-biodegradable polymers from more than one country of origin, with your individual personalised name clearly printed on the front in a bold modern user-friendly script, and is professionally designed to be opened with the teeth, or, for those with dentures/wonky bridgework/cold sores, any other handy sharp implement (not supplied). NB: Take care to stand well away from other people or pets when pulling the catalogue out, since an elbow in the eye may offend. Should a child/cat/uncaged bird get its head inside the envelope, pull it off. (The envelope, not the head: if the latter is what you inadvertently do, consult your GP or any reliable vet as soon as possible. Please note that the catalogue-makers are not responsible for any damage or injury arising, including a staple in the thumb/lip/other soft tissue. While every effort is made to secure all sharp components to avoid making holes in you, be advised that staples can go up as well as down.)

Before you open your luxury catalogue to partake of the boundless joys within, take just a moment to savour the handsome cover. Embracing beauty and practicality, it has been fashioned from a bespoke glossy paper which may be personally wiggled about to reflect all sorts of light – sun, bedside lamp, chandelier, powerful torch, or even a big candle – and artist-designed to confer the immense pleasure which may be derived from examining, in your own home, absolutely free, two delightful teddy bears pulling a glistening cracker in front of a fireplace decked with boughs of holly in which a mysterious snow-covered boot may be glimpsed descending.

Opening the catalogue – which has been cleverly constructed so as to be operable to both left- and right-handed users – you will notice that each magnificent full-colour life-size page is equipped with its own individual number, expertly chosen to correspond to the page it is on, in elegant time-honoured numerals. Lowering your head to partake of the joy of these more closely, you will be amazed to discover that the page you are perusing gives off a wondrous fragrance which superbly complements its rich silky feel. This antique-style odour is put in at the secret location where the no-expense-spared printing is carried out by skilled hands which have been passed on from father to son for countless generations. (Caution: while every attempt has been made to ensure that these voluptuous pages are allergen-free, it is possible – in just a very few cases – that prolonged and/or deep sniffing may cause sneezing, eye-watering, or a rash. If symptoms persist, consult a qualified specialist, or dial 999, where you will be swiftly put through to a team of specially trained operators standing by, day and night, to deal with valued customers who may have caught something off a catalogue.)

And now it is time to savour what is actually to be found on these pages, starting with the copious original illustrations commissioned from a myriad of top-of-the-range photographers who have pooled their genius to bring you (following hours of painstaking selection by major experts, many with fine university degrees in this sort of work) a truly breathtaking range of captivating pictures so diverse that only an exclusive Christmas gift catalogue can offer them to a discerning clientele prepared to be thrilled by their incomparability. Be it a charming snap of a winsome Yorkie modelling monogrammed dogs' boots, a dramatic landscape depicting snow-sprinkled Buddhas of various sizes holding cork-extruders for relaxed al fresco drinking (bottles not included), an intimate study of a car-cover in flame-proof Nepalese candlewick, or a dramatically lit portrait of an onyx haddock singing one of three Scottish lullabies (please state which when ordering), every picture tells a story you and your loved ones will never tire of hearing. And as if all this were not enough, beneath each graphic masterpiece you will find an exquisite paragraph fashioned, just for you, from a plenitude of hand-wrought words fully guaranteed to be unavailable anywhere else.

Wall Game

YES, you are not wrong, I am back. As a matter of fact, I am as back as it is possible for me to be. I am up a ladder leaning against my back wall. I am not here in order to say 'hello, wall, I am back, too, I missed you', I am not even up here to thank the wall for the terrific job it did in protecting the house that the wall is at the back of, I am up here because I have come back to discover that the terrific job it did is in jeopardy. I am up here because I have been asked to sack the wall, and I wanted to run my hand along the top of it just to make sure of something before I let fly at the people who want to take my back wall's livelihood away. I intend to fight to save its job.

It has being doing that job unswervingly for nigh on 200 years. I say unswervingly, but it has, not surprisingly, grown a bit buckled in service, it has lost its ruddy youth, it has got mossy, it has been nibbled away by this climbing creeper and that, but as for the climbers it was formally employed to keep out, it has never failed: it has deterred Regency footpads and Jack the Ripper, it has seen off all three Krays and Osama bin Laden, it has taken it upon itself to reassure Mrs Coren and me and all who preceded us down the long arches of the criminal years that we may pick up our buckets and spades with a light and carefree heart and decamp to wherever in the world our fancies took us, in the sure and certain knowledge that our premises were in the safe hands of our back wall.

That is because it has broken glass along the top. It is very old glass: this is a back wall you could lorry onto the

Antiques Road Show to bring the serried experts whimpering gratefully to their knees. But now the council wants me to chisel it off: I have just arrived home to discover among the teetering pile of mail a curt note informing me that the glass on my back wall constitutes a danger to anyone who might want to climb over it. Which is why I have come down off the ladder, now, and into the house, and vaulted over the bags that Mrs Coren is unpacking – silently, because the years have taught her not to ask a man why he has brought only one sandal back when he has, without even a sidelong glance, hurtled past a screen on which South Africa has just lost its eighth wicket for only 81, this is a man with priorities – grabbed a telephone and begun letting myself be bounced from one to another of 183 different departments which would not exist without my heavy subsidy until I at last find myself in contact with a prong who explains that the glass-on-wall initiative is part of the ongoing policy of care in the community. Broken glass on top of a wall could mean that someone might get hurt.

I am very patient with him. My voice is hardly more than a shriek when it points out that I am the community and what I care about is someone who might get hurt when there is no glass on top of a wall to stop hurters from climbing in. For this I get a literally sharp answer: the prong suggests a prickly shrub. I observe that it would take a prickly shrub ten years to grow to deterrent height, does he appreciate how many household chattels could disappear over the course of 4000 days and nights? By 2013 I might not have even one sandal to stand up in, and anyway, what is the difference between a villain cutting his hand on a bit of beer-bottle and poking his eye out on a thorn, is there an ongoing policy about organically grown sharp things? But he merely invites me to ring my local

Crime Prevention Officer; who says, yes, a glass-topped wall could be construed as an offensive weapon, and when I reply that I would be prepared to sign a piece of paper promising not to pick my wall up and chase a burglar down the street with it, insists that this is a serious matter, I could well find myself in trouble if a thief were hurt on my premises. He does not elaborate, but hanging in the air between us, I can tell, is the reminder that Tony Martin has recently left a cell vacant, Mrs Coren could soon be repacking my bag.

Where might this not end? I do not tell him I have coated my drainpipes with slippery paint – it is possible that a second-storey man might not make it past the first floor, break his ankle, and leave the courts to decide which of us gets six months – nor that my burglar alarm is a bit loud, it could quite literally frighten the life out of a villain with a dodgy ticker, nor that I have a sash-window that comes down, uninvited, at a hell of a lick and could easily leave an intruder's head rolling around on my bedroom carpet. I merely thank him, and ring off, because I have been up the ladder and I know two things. I know that my broken glass is very old, and I know that this is a listed building, and no one may touch a hair of its heritage fabric without asking the freeholder's permission. The freeholder is the Crown. I intend to do nothing. The council may write to the Queen, if it has the bottle.

Smart Money

FREE internet access, we read, means such parlous times for academic books that publishers are suggesting corporate subsidy. This bothers me: hardbacks may well fall prey to kickbacks . . .

From: *PATHOLOGY OF MARSUPIAL MUSCULATURE*

'. . . come now to the most specialised of the wallabies, the *Petrogale,* or Rock Wallaby. These have feet adapted to their habitat and tails employed solely as balancing organs, not for the purpose of advancing the animal in the more familiar 'tripod' progression.

Thus, the Rock Wallaby may take up to 15.7 seconds to move from rest to 30mph, i.e. far slower than even the cheapest Datsubishi in the 2007 range, the elegant yet economical Loganberry 1.3, which is further distinguished from the Rock Wallaby by having, *as standard fitments,* heated wing-mirrors, fog-light, sat-nav, William Tell hooter, and luminous hot beverage holder! Incredible, cry top zoologists, how do they do it for only £8,799?

Lacking a fog-light, the Rock Wallaby is at an unquestionable disadvantage in murky weather, when it could easily jump straight into a tree and drop any hot beverage it happened to be carrying. Furthermore, unlike the Loganberry, the Rock Wallaby will not hold its secondhand value, due in no small measure to the durability of the car's chic Nippotex upholstery. In tests, nine out of ten zoologists could not tell Nippotex from Rock

Wallaby fur, and were amazed when the commonest Rock Wallaby parasite, *Siphonaptera nausica,* or rectal flea, jumped in their hundreds from the marsupial's pelt into the Nippotex and began breeding enthusiastically. As for servicing . . .'

From: *COMING OF AGE IN MELANESIA*

'. . . selects the bride of his choice by sticking his finger in her ear, and mimicking the cry of the toadhawk.

The rest of the village then pelt the couple with nuptial loaves baked in the shape of external genitalia, and bring the bride-to-be decorated packages containing everything from ox curd and tooth-paint to rattan room-dividers and ape-face pillows.

To set these rituals in an illustrative context, it is not unlike having a wedding list at Harridges, the store globally renowned for quality and service. Whereas the lusty Koi-Koi warrior sticks his finger in his beloved's ear, the young Englishman visiting the superb Knightsbridge jewellery department will find a breathtaking range of engagement rings to suit every taste. These are not, of course, to be stuck in the ear. As for the gift needs of guests, while they will not find festive loaves or bits of ape, there are amazing bargains in Waterford crystal, table lighters (for lighting cigarettes, not tables), Irish linen, doorchimes, personalised stationery, and – a particular Harridge feature – pouffes of every kind. And just as the Koi-Koi father will shrink the head of his new daughter-in-law's least favourite . . .'

Radio Fun

TODAY is a really big day. That is why I have just finished servicing and polishing my father's old Ferguson. See how it gleams! Savour how it smells!

Hear how it thunders when I start it up!

I haven't given my old man's Ferguson such a seeing to in the 15 years since he died, when I took it from his place and brought it to mine. I should say here (since it has just occurred to me that unlikely pictures may be forming in your mind's eye), that it is not an old Ferguson tractor, it is an old Ferguson wireless. It was given to my parents as a wedding present in 1935, and a very snazzy present it was; I stress this only because younger readers may think of a wireless, if they even know the word, as a titchy plastic box you clip onto your belt for jogging. They may never have seen a walnut and rosewood number the size and simulacrum of a Sheraton sideboard, standing on four sturdy cabriole legs, with six brass knobs on the front to fine-tune three enormous dials that glow in three different colours to let you know they're in business, we are Long, Short and Medium, sir, begging your pardon, sir, and we are here to serve you, we await your pleasure, sir, you have only to twiddle. It is a wireless worth getting married for.

And, culturally speaking (which it did), it brought me up. For the first dozen years of my life, much of what I learned and most of what I enjoyed came to me through this huge speaker cunningly fretworked into, for some reason, a spray of roses. Even after 1950, when my old man bought a TV set as big as a wardrobe (whose giant oak doors nevertheless revealed a screen as big as a fag-packet), thereby so filling our little front room with electronic carpentry that only two people could ever watch or listen at a time, the third having to stand in the hall, it was the radio that did the business. Not only did it teach me more of this and that (though not, in those Reithian times, the other) than any schoolteacher ever did, it also entertained me better than anyone I ever knew: it seamlessly graduated me from *Uncle Mac* and *Toytown* and *Just William* and *Norman and Henry Bones* – subtitled *The Boy Detectives,* despite the fact that Norman was queenie old Charles Hawtrey and Henry was matronly old Marjorie Westbury, a weekly *Radio Times* revelation that not only never bothered me at all, but probably did much to explain the infinitely elastic unbigotry for which I am a byword today – to *Take It From Here* and *The Goon Show* and *Ray's A Laugh* and *Hancock's Half-Hour* and all the myriad other comic masterpieces from the Golden Age of Ears.

I look at the Ferguson now, and I hear it then. See these three dials? Clock not only all the poignantly yesteryear Anglophone stations, Hilversum and Daventry, Allouis and Athlone, and, yes, Valetta and Cairo – there is a map of the world on the back of the set, faded now but still half pink where once it was half red – but also Oslo and Ankara and Prague and Paris and Breslau and many a polyglottal dozen more. Oft in the stilly night, I used to creep past the door rattling in concert with my old man's nostrils, and pad downstairs, and switch the Ferguson on, and wait while the dials began slowly to glow and the valves to hum and the speaker to whistle as I spun the dial in search of microphones a thousand crackling miles across the night. I learnt a lot of French that way, and doubtless no small smattering, now sadly lost, of Lapp and Urdu.

It was, of course, only mine exclusively in the wee small hours: in the huge large ones, it served all three of us. Sometimes in pairs: since it took two people to move it so that my mother would have room to put up the ironing-board, I would occasionally hang around to listen to Mrs Dale's Diary; tricky for her, because, though she enjoyed having me there, the script would from time to time daringly offer a mildly gynaecological moment, and my mother dreaded questions. Care for another pairing? Me sitting with my old man as the football results came in and he checked his pools coupon, not because I chose to but because my mother knew if I was there he wouldn't swear.

But the proper pairing for today is one I didn't join. It was just them. You know why today is a really big day? Because it is Neville Chamberlain's birthday. If he were alive today he'd be 134, and people would pay good money to look at him, but when he was 70, what people did was listen to him. And it was on this Ferguson that he told my parents that no such undertaking had been received and in consequence this country was at war. Which is why I have fettled it. I rather fear it is time to switch it on again.

A Bit On The Side

EXCITED by the interview in Monday's *Times* with H. Cameron Barnes, here from America to promote his self-help book *Affair!*, thousands of you have written to ask me whether there is similar aid for British adulterers eager to kick over the marital traces without being found out. Alert to your every need, I have plucked a few forbidden fruit from the Internet . . .

RUBBER BRIDGE. Despite the most meticulous timing and calculations, many men, having slipped from the nuptial sack after the wife has dropped off in mid-headache, find they are unable to return to it from their little friend's apartment before dawn breaks. Why not avoid those dangerous crosstown dashes by bridging your absence with the sensational My Old Man? My Old Man is, when inflated, a full-size husband: you simply slide out of bed, slide My Old Man in, carefully pump him up, stick his head under your pillow, and leave. Should you return after sun-up, your wife will notice nothing! While she is cooking your breakfast, you can slip back covertly, deflate My Old Man in seconds, and saunter downstairs without a care in the world. Order NOW from PO Box 18, Tring, only £49.95 (pyjamas not included).

CHERCHEZ LA FEMME. Hot flushes are a common female complaint, often brought on by the question: 'What did you do today, I tried to ring you?' Now you can exchange that blush for a smug smile! Our brilliant RUN OFF MY FEET COMPENDIUM offers women a fabulous range of watertight alibis, including two Tupperware buckets, ten used bingo cards, four plastic bags (Safeway, Liberty, Ikea, Bergdorf Goodman), six Odeon stubs, three dental appointment notices, two failed MoT certificates, a soiled and numbered marathon vest, a black veil and armband, and a Cordon Bleu diploma on genuine vellumette with your name embossed in gold!

Ring 083971 66547 for details. No salesman will call, unless you fancy a big Greek plumber with liquid eyes and a skin like watered silk.

DO YOU REQUIRE a full-colour set of professional photographs of your affair, handsomely bound and mailed by us to relatives and friends? If the answer is no, then a cheque for £1000, popped in the post right this minute, will instantly dissuade our crack team of paparazzi from springing out on you (or in on you) in the small hours. SNAP DECISIONS, 4a, Grole House, SW9 3HH.

DIAMONDS ARE FOREVER – which could well be acutely embarrassing. What you should be after is something that says Thank You My Darling and rots without trace as soon as possible. For example, why not a psittacosis-riddled macaw? A mere £750, yet it shrieks 'I love you, I love you, I love you' over and over again for several hours, before dropping dead. Or perhaps your own effigy in Neapolitan ice-cream, decorated with erotic messages in little silver balls which fall off into illegibility after five minutes at room temperature, only £50 (hot fudge sauce extra)?
Don't delay, e-mail today, to syd@briefencounters.co.uk

FULL MARKS! Nothing is more likely to rock an otherwise sensible, practical, and numbingly boring marriage than the sudden sight, on one partner or the other, of inexplicable bruises, carpet-burns, toothmarks, weals, or scratches. Now you can make them explicable with a wide range of pills and ointments whose labels clearly state that the bottles contain antidotes for snakebite, old Turkish remedies for bubonic plague, oral anti-tetanus vaccine for barbed wire wounds, etc. The contents vary from cold cream to Smarties, and start at only £7.95 from Placebo Domingo Ltd, Suitcase 9, Oxford Street, W1.

NEED A FULL-LENGTH VIDEO of a major Hong Kong sales conference so ineptly shot, wrongly focused, wobbly, and under-exposed as to render all human figures unrecognisable?

Should you require this incontrovertible proof that your spouse was utterly out of order in suspecting you of actually being shacked up in the Bide-a-Wee Motel, Galashiels, during those eight days, we should be delighted to supply it under plain cover to your nominated post restante. Also available: Desert Rats Reunion, Geneva Motor Show, Highland Games, UKIP Seminar, Solo Transatlantic Yacht Race, and many more. From £250. WRITE: Who? Me? Films, 8 Pondicherry Crescent, Uxbridge.

A Nose By Any Other Name Would Smell As Sweet

I HAVE just spent several days looking for a new nose. Do not, however, jump to cruel conclusions about the webhunting of cosmetic rhinopractors: a glance at my back-flap mugshot, if you can bear it, should quickly tell you that a new nose wouldn't help; nothing short of a whole head replacement could sort things out, so until the window-boxes of Harley Street are in a position to offer a full range of fetching transplantables waving on genetically modified sunflower stalks and awaiting the open chequebooks of the vain, I fear I shall be forced to stick with what Mother Nature delivered to Mother Coren. The new nose I was looking for was not for me, but for Aphrodite.

It had to be a very small nose, mind, for she is a very small Aphrodite. A pocket Venus. She is only three feet tall, though terribly attractive, if you like conkless women, and I picked her up at a country sale a week ago for a knockdown price, probably because she had at some point in her statuary career been knocked down, leaving her nose where she fell. I do not know where that was, otherwise I should go round and look for it, even though the likelihood is that the nose is no longer there: it would have been a pretty nose, I imagine, given that its owner is the goddess of beauty, so someone coming across it, wherever it was that it lay bodiless, would have been bound to pocket it and take it home to put on the mantelpiece. Then again, if all this happened a long time ago, and the finder were a toff, it might well have ended up on his watch-chain; it would be an interesting talking point, should you run out of things to say about Home Rule or the new Trollope, and it would make small grandchildren giggle whenever you plucked it out of your waistcoat pocket and swung it.

Anyway, wherever the nose is now, it wasn't on the little stone coquette I ported home from Wiltshire to put in my garden. Mrs Coren insisted this didn't matter, distress was part of its charm, not to mention its mystery, look at the Sphinx, but my view was that a statue designed to celebrate feminine perfection wasn't doing its job if it appeared to have gone three rounds with Mike Tyson, and as far as mystery was concerned, I would rather not have people coming into my garden and saying what's that, why's it got no nose, does it do riddles?

So I turned, as I invariably do when the chips are down (and this being, for once, quite literally the case) to the *Yellow Pages*, to find, astonishingly, that there was nothing between non-ferrous metals and notaries. Which drove me and my PC into the hands of Google, Sherlock and Jeeves – who could easily be a firm of notaries but are in fact discrete search engines – and when I tell you that though between them they came up with umpteen entries for nose, many so extravagantly repellent that I shall never again be able to look into a handkerchief without fear and trembling, none of them had the faintest idea of where I might get hold of a stone one. Jeeves, to be fair, did shimmer in with long lists of both stonemasons and sculpture restorers, but it didn't take many phone calls to discover that no mason was prepared to unsheath his chisel for anything so titchy, and that the only way to get a restorer to give you a nose was to give him an arm and a leg.

So, yesterday, I decided to build one. I stood Aphrodite on the garden table so that our faces were of a height, I mixed the Polyfilla to the prescribed formula, I pressed the lump to the stump, and while it was still pliable, I shaped it with care and, yes, love. You will say, that was a tad risky, remember Pygmalion, Mrs Coren would not take kindly to coming out into the garden and discovering that you had fallen head-over-heels for a Greek midget, but you are wrong; when Mrs Coren came into the garden, what she said was: 'What is the Duke of Wellington doing on the table?' So I tried to tweak a bit off the end of the nose, but it wasn't pliable any more, it was crumbly, and I had to start again, this time moulding a selection of noses, retrousse, button, flared, something I'd spotted on Jennifer Lopez, but let me tell you it isn't easy, you get the nose right and then try to poke nostrils in with a twig and the whole thing suddenly goes bulbous, you are looking at Sid James, but I managed it, finally, and I carried Aphrodite to a shady spot beneath an apple tree. Where her nose soon dried to – Mrs Coren helpfully pointed out – a slightly different colour from her head.

'It'll weather in', I said.

But it didn't. It weathered off. Either that, or a bird stood on it. When we looked out this morning, Aphrodite and her nose were side by side. 'Not exactly aphrodisiac, is it?' I said. 'Shall I bin it?' 'No,' said Mrs Coren, 'look on the bright side. It's a terrific memento mori.'

Regime Change

COUNTLESS workaholic readers with no time for gyms or marathons have e-mailed me following Monday's mould-breaking news from applied physiologist Professor Martin Gibala that all a 24/7 nose-grinder needs to achieve tip-top fitness is just two minutes a day using either a cycling machine or a folding bike kept in the boot of the car. They want to know if this regime really works. It does. I have been there.

Here you are, driving to the office. Too often, busy-busy people like you make the car an excuse for letting up on exercise, but trust me, umpteen opportunities abound for working out that flabby old body of yours as you drive. First, keep a constant eye open for fitness freaks who have already unfolded their bicycles: they will, as part of their workout, overtake you on the inside, shoot across you on the red light, cut in without signalling, spit, scream, give you the finger, and bang their fists on your roof. Do not let them outfitness you: jam on your brakes (firming up ankles), grip the wheel until your fingers go white (shedding unsightly knuckle-fat), scream back even more hysterically (toning up wattle-necks), give them two fingers to their one (strengthening digital sinew), and bang your own fist on the dashboard (accelerating heart-rate and dislodging dangerous platelets).

Next, try to text your congestion-charge number: 500 rapid press-ups will give you a thumb of iron, and, since you still cannot get through, hurling your cellphone out of the window will boost wrist-sinew, especially if, in your invaluable cholesterol-thinning rage, you have forgotten to open it, allowing the cellphone to bounce back onto the rear seat, compelling groping and flailing just great for arms, neck and shoulders.

Nearing your office, be sure to take advantage of the fact that the congestion charge doesn't work: park a mile away, remove your folding bicycle from the boot, and attempt to put it together. I have frequently found that throwing a partly assembled folding bicycle into the road and screaming as you jump up and down on it gets the whole body working. You can feel it in your temples. Now you have broken it, you are in a splendid position to jog – carrying your muscle-building briefcase, lap-top, overcoat, umbrella, and gunny-sack of healthy lunch-time yak-yoghurt and fibrous growths from more than one country of origin – to the nearest department store, to buy a cycling machine instead.

Once there, and the sweat has dried from pores so healthily opened you can poke a pencil through them, remember to take the lift, NOT the stairs. It's a mistake so many keep-fit fanatics make: stairs will strengthen only adipose legs and hips, but a lift which insists on going up when you pressed down, ensures that you are stuck behind three women with pushchairs and a man with a new garden bench when the doors eventually open at your floor but shut again before you can push through, and may even, with any luck, pack up altogether between floors, will enable you to jump up and down, wave your arms about, bang on the doors, fall to your knees, open all those lucky pores again, and, most important, get those sluggish lungs and heart of yours working overtime, never mind toughening your bladder no end.

You will need the lift because, having asked on the ground floor if they sell exercise bikes, you will be directed to the enquiry desk on the top floor, who will advise you try the sports department in the basement, where everyone will be (a) off sick with RSI, (b) seeing their lawyer about the till which caused it, (c) on maternity leave, or (d) taking a counselling break – with the sole exception of a Finn brought up in Taiwan, the battery of whose hearing-aid has just gone flat. You will both run around for a while, pulling out croquet sets and fishing rods and ping-pong bats, until his colleague returns from counselling and, summoning all the English you would expect from a Chinese brought up in Finland, directs you to the fifth floor. Which will turn out to be Ye Olde Nigella Burger Bar and Staff Infirmary, where a fist-faced matron will send you back to the enquiry desk in the attic.

Great, or what? Having galloped many a mile, shed many a kilo, and fettled everything attached to your skeleton and hanging inside it, don't you feel fighting fit? Now do something for someone else: buy the bike and take it to the office, so your mates can see it. Laughter is the best medicine.

On A Wing And A Prayer

LOUIS Bleriot; Charles Lindbergh; Douglas Bader; Guy Gibson; the Red Coren. Every generation has one. Welcome aboard, this is your ace speaking. We shall be flying at 30,000 feet at a speed of 550 mph, just as soon as the kid stops screaming. Until the kid stops screaming, we have no way of knowing if the engines are working. For your information, the engines on this Boeing 767 are RR RB 211-524Hs. Rolls-Royce are very proud of them: at 550 mph all you can hear is the ticking of the clock. Unless the kid is screaming. If the kid is screaming, you couldn't hear Big Ben.

The kid is across the aisle from me, in an ordinary seat. I am in a very special seat. Not only is it very special, it is also very important. It is what we flying aces call the bulkhead exit seat. It has more leg room than ordinary economy seats, it has more leg room than club class seats, that is why we flying aces always check in by telephone before we fly, but that is not what makes it important. What makes it important is that in the event of an emergency, we aces have to do the thing with the big handle that opens the emergency door, and we have to help with the chute; we have to make sure passengers have removed their high heels, spectacles, and teeth, and, if they have a thing about sharks and do not want to go down the chute, we have to throw them out. If sharks do turn up, we have to dive in and knock them about. That is why we have to be fit: when we check in, the deskman on the telephone asks us how fit we are. We tell him terrifically fit: like well-oiled machines – which we intend to be as soon as the booze trolley comes round, that is one of the reasons we need the extra leg room, we want to stretch out and zizz after we have drunk the trolley – we rattle off our pulse-rate, blood pressure, cholesterol level, body mass index, glucose tolerance, hearing/vision factors, press-ups per day, all that. Fit or what?

So then, Sunday night, Nice airport, soft damson sunset over the adjacent Med, the Boeing has taxied to its take-off point, the stewardess is about to do the emergency drill, and the kid is smiling happily beside his, I guess, daddy. He is two years old, and he is an angel: he looks like Millais' Bubbles. Pears soap wouldn't melt in his mouth. At this point the stewardess snaps open the yellow life jacket, slips it on, and sticks the oxygen mask over her face. And the kid goes crazy. No kid ever screamed like it. No adult ever screamed like it. He is only a small kid, but his body must be made up entirely of tonsil. Never mind not hearing the engines, if the kid doesn't stop screaming soon the windows will shatter. The tyres will burst. The electronics will fuse. Alerted fire-tenders and anti-terrorist APCs will come clanging and howling towards us – though we shall, of course, not be able to hear them. The stewardess is staring at the kid, the kid is shrieking at the stewardess, and economy passengers fore and aft are straining in their seat belts to try to clock what's happening: could be an ullulating fundamentalist about to claim his six dozen virgins, could be a turbine blade shearing through an engine, could be a shark attack – maybe they're getting bolder, like foxes, hurtling out of the Baie des Anges, who knows? – could be anything, this is 2007 and this is a plane. I glance past the stewardess at the club class curtain; it is trembling. Rich people up front, free caviare, free foie gras, have no inkling what might be happening back here: are the poor people, no free caviare, no free foie gras, eating a kid?

The kid's daddy is distraught. He picks up the kid, but it is like picking up a dervish octopus, the kid is flailing, a left hook, a right jab, teeth, flying snot, the yellow-jacketed stewardess steps towards them, the tonsils go up to warp-factor decibels, the fuselage might crack . . . and it is at this point that the ace intervenes. This is his moment: it is for this that not only all his fitness has prepared him, but also his incomparable savvy. He tells the stewardess that it is the yellow jacket which has detonated the kid. She takes it off, but the kid does not stop screaming, he is not fooled, there is a monster aboard, this is a fee-fi-fo-fum moment, but the ace is not fazed, he has a trump left to play before push comes to shove and he has to open the door and fire the kid down the shute. He tells the stewardess to blow her whistle. The stewardess frowns. You know how to whistle, don't you, says the ace, you put your lips together and you blow into that thing dangling from the life jacket. The stewardess replies that this is only for emergencies, but the ace – fit, cool, authorative – says: what do you think this is?

So she picks up the whistle, and blows. It is a hell of whistle: the kid stops. He has met his match. It is all over. The plane takes off. The ace settles back into the special seat he was born to fill. Eat his shorts, Biggles.

Chocs Away

TOMORROW is a major day. It is the last day of an era. The midnight chimes which gong on May 1 will herald a watershed between romance and lust. I know this, because Nestlé tells me so. They have clearly chosen their day with much forethought: May 1 has been a watershed between romance and lust since time immoral, for it is the day when maidens wake up to deck themselves with flowers and dance around a tall signifier designed to ensure that as soon as they have finished dancing they will be chased giggling into the long grass and comprehensively undecked.

Now, Nestlé make a signifier, too, albeit not so tall. Just six inches. It is built by stacking 11 circular chocolate-covered caramels on top of one another. Here is a press release about it: 'Rolo's famous chocolate slogan of 'Do you love anyone enough to give them your last Rolo?' is being axed after 23 years because makers Nestlé think it too romantic to reflect modern relationships. It will be replaced on May 1 by advertisements in which an office girl flashes her underwear to get one of the sweets, because Nestlé research shows that romance is not the most important thing in a modern relationship. It's time to move on.'

Time to move on whom is not of course specified, but we can be sure it will not stop at office girls. If Nestlé has its marketing strategy in line, you may be confident that, after May 1, the sassy female spectrum from Ulrika Johnsson to Margaret Beckett will be leaning fetchingly against the water-cooler, murmuring: 'Is that a tube of Rolo in your pocket or are you just pleased to see me?' You may be sure, too, that there will be equally naff observations from the lads along the lines of: 'The trouble with a tube of Rolo is that after you give her one, it gets smaller.' You know how people are, these days.

But you also know me, and you will therefore know that I am a little uneasy about all this, not least (pretend I care) on Nestlé's behalf. The exchange of chocolates for women may have an ancient provenance, but I surely cannot be alone in finding it somewhat iffy. It can so easily backfire. In the romantic lang syne, when it was a truth universally acknowledged that a single man in possession of a box of Black Magic must be in want of a wife, I fell in love with great regularity. In consequence, even in my teens, I was frequently to be found sliding five bob across the Woollies' confectionery counter in the hope of securing, later that same day, the first Mrs Coren. I was not after anything else: picture me as that sad jerk in a black jumpsuit who used to parachute onto the north face of the Eiger, abseil down through a thunderstorm, swim across the icy lake at the bottom, break and enter a lakeside house via the bedroom window, leave a little carton on a bedside table, and then, in major italics, clear off again, without even looking in the bed to see if he could learn something to his advantage. All because the lady loved Milk Tray. And, subtextually, all because she was a lady. Leaving us to assume that, after he had delivered the requisite number of chocolates and had a word with her father, she married him.

I did a lot of that, in my search for romance, not so much in the Alps as in the Southgate Odeon – a spot no less hazardous if, for example, all you could afford that week was Maltesers, which, lovingly placed in the lap beside you, could easily, if its new owner was startled, say, by a hand suddenly clamping her far shoulder, fly off and send its contents rolling down to the front. You got blamed for that. You often walked home alone. Worse yet, I fell deeply in love with a number of future Mrs Corens in tooth-braces, several of whom got bits of hazelnut cluster lodged in their canines, to the terminal detriment of advanced kissing. More than once, too, I would reach out romantically for a hand that already had half an unwanted coffee-creme in it. From which you will understand when I say that bartering chocolates for wives, even in those pre-feminist days, wasn't all that the advertisers cracked it up to be. (Just as, a little later, I was to discover what a scam candle-lit dinners were: fine at the start, when the candles were tall, but as they burned down to below chin height, the person opposite you turned into an uplit ghost train ghoul. Also, your nostrils had to be spotless.)

So then, what happens after May 1, when Nestlé will be offering not romance for chocs, but sex? If men are led to believe that there are dames out there eager to flash their underwear for just one Rolo, what will they expect from those prepared to take on the whole first eleven? Will it, as it so often did under the old regime, all end it tears? Maybe not: these are, after all, different times. Love is only a Rolo in the hay.

Green Thoughts

I THINK I have contracted compulsive–obsessive disorder, if it is called that. It may be called obsessive– compulsive disorder, or, indeed, something else entirely, but in order to pin down what it is, I should have to get up from the computer on which I am tapping this and go across to the bookshelves and try to look up whatever it is that it is, and that would mean putting the light on, because it is midnight as I write, and I can't put the light on because of what I have contracted. I am tapping only by the light of the screen.

I know how I contracted it, mind. I caught it off my carbon footprint. Or, rather, my carbon shadow, because it is not just under my shoe, it is stuck to me at all points. Like you, I never thought about it until very recently, but now I cannot think about anything else, which also means that I cannot do anything without thinking about it.

This morning, I couldn't think how to shave, because I have both a safety and an electric razor. Which is worse for the planet? The electric sucks from a fossily power station, the safety is made of steel and non-biodegradable plastic which will end up on a landfill site, possibly cutting a gull's throat to boot, with God knows what ecological consequences.

And when I recall cleaning my teeth, the tremors start all over again. I have an electric water pick for flushing old dinner out at dawn, but I daren't use it any more. I would have to plant a tree. I do not know where you get these trees you have to plant every time you burn carbon, but I bet you have to drive there, and you would have to buy another tree to offset the petrol. I can't do that every morning, especially as I have a very small garden. In less than a week, it would be a very small forest. Its roots would gobble up the water table and the house would fall over.

Which leads me to my non-electric toothbrushing: it wasted ten times more water than the water pick would have done, because we had pork belly last night, and most of it was still wedged between my molars. The brushing also used a lot of energy (mine) and that doesn't grow on trees: or, rather, does, given that I got the energy from the protein which Mrs Coren cooked last night with gas made from what might well have borne conkers, once.

Mind you, I had already used most of that energy before bedtime. I had to take the rubbish out to umpteen different eco-categories of bin, but I wouldn't put the garden lights on to do it, obviously, and the bottom fell out of one of the wet paper sacks we now use instead of planetocidal plastic, so I had to crawl around in the dark burning up precious pig, and when I finally got back indoors, Mrs Coren had turned off the telly standby light, and my disorder wouldn't let me turn it on again to watch the cricket highlights.

However, if England ever get another whiff of the Ashes – and how non-sustainable is that? – I think I could manage, just the once, to force one compulsive obsession to override another. Even if it cost a tree or two.

Sea Fever

Mrs Coren and I have reached that happy point in life where we get asked out a lot. Fat glossy invitations plop daily to our mat. Some kind hosts want us to join them for an invigorating game of shuffleboard in the Bosporus, to be followed by a jolly sing-song in their candle-scented sauna; others insist we come with them to camcord penguins, and, when darkness foils the straining lens, foxtrot the night away to the internationally renowned melodies of Morrie Plunk and his Mandoliers. More yet beg us to island-hop with them from one Maldive to the next, tantalisingly dangling the promise of a dinghy whose transparent bottom will allow us, while sipping sundown cocktails shielded from gnats by titchy parasols, to gawp at turtles.

Of course, there will be a price to pay. That is how cruises work. And they work better at it with every passing day as more and more OAPs pluck equity from the stratosphere into which their properties have soared and grope creakily for their cruisewear. It is why, last Sunday, the *Liberty of the Seas*, the hugest liner ever built, hove to off Southampton on its first promotional trip. Know what it was promoting? Not merely its malls, cinemas, casinos, pubs, ballrooms, swimming-pools, and all the other gewgaws of common or garden cruiseboats, but also its common or garden, which boasts a running-track, an ice-rink, a nine-hole golf course, a waterfall, and a cliff-face to enable rock-climbers to keep their hand, or at least their fingertips, in.

Not, I'm afraid, my idea of a ship; my idea of Basingstoke. I write this because, yes, Mrs Coren and I did receive an invitation, and this piece will save us the bother of a formal reply. Thanks, but we shall not be sailing off to shop, filmgo, bet, booze, boogie, swim, sprint, skate, negotiate the tricky dog-leg fourth, go over the falls in a barrel, or up the north face of anything, because if we did want to do that we would not elect to do it on a prison-hulk, however swish; for that is not what ships are about.

And they are about to be about even less. Soon, you may be sure, there will be a *Diabolical Liberty of the Seas*, ten times the size of this one, its lucky passengers living in thatched cottages, fishing the trout-lake, playing cricket, riding to hounds, and taking luxury trains to the afterdeck to watch Saracens v. Wasps; but Mrs Coren and I will not be sailing with them.

If we ever accept an invitation to sail anywhere, it will have to come from a seafaring man with one leg we meet in an inn, whose lugger lies straining at its hawser, canvas furled, waiting to ship us and his parrot round the howling Horn for a few pieces of eight, weevils our only dining experience, rum our only sundown tipple, a concertina our only dance-band, and our only gamble the outside chance of finding an uncharted island where x marks the spot.

And if our only fellow guests are fifteen men on a dead man's chest, that's fine with us.

Anything Legal Considered

THE Law Society is right to observe that 'in our burgeoning blame culture, it is to be expected that some plaintiffs who become mired in litigation may have only themselves to blame.' For who could blame the lawyers when, every day, my postbag sags beneath the weight of letters like this?

Dear Mr Coren:
In June 1994, a tree root from next door's garden grew through the side of our new polystyrene pond, causing serious subsidence to a gnome. My neighbour refused compensation, so my solicitor sought counsel's advice. He recommended I go to court, where the case took nine days, because of a number of what my counsel described as fascinatingly unforeseeable legal points, several dating back to 1326, and I lost. Costs ran to five figures.

Being short of money, I sought time to pay, and took a second job as a nightwatchman, where I was laid out by a baseball bat. The company sacked me for incompetence, and counsel insisted I sue for unfair dismissal. At the hearing, evidence was admitted from the trial of the batter, who had been found not guilty on the grounds that I had shouted at him aggressively when he broke the door down and caused him the emotional distress for which I had been forced to compensate him, so the dismissal was upheld. Costs were given against me. They were also given against me in the case my solicitor advised me to bring against my other employer, who had dismissed me from my day job on the grounds that I had been off work for two weeks attending a hearing about being unfairly dismissed from my second job.

Now unemployed, I could not find work due to pains in my batted head. My barrister sought compensation, but this was denied because a previous court had ruled that I had brought the injury on myself by aggressive shouting. To pay my lawyers' bills for all this I had to sell my house, but I did not get as much as I hoped because of the legal fees involved, and since my wife did not fancy living over a chip shop, she sued for divorce.

My lawyers recommended I defend the suit, which I lost, costs awarded to my wife, and as I left the court I tripped on a broken kerb and dislocated my hip. My lawyers instantly initiated a negligence suit against Westminster Council, who not only won but also successfully counterclaimed for making the kerb worse than it was before.

When my hip repair went wrong, the Medical Defence Union, acting for the surgeon I was advised to sue for negligence, employed three QCs, but I, being bankrupt, had to defend myself. The case took a month, due to all the hours I spent limping to and fro across the court as witness and counsel, until it was time to cash in my pension fund to pay the MDU costs.

What I want to know is: if I could get a loan from those nice people who advertise on television, would you advise me to sue my lawyers?

Dial M For Money

NOW, viewers, before we go into the commercial break and the final part of this week's riveting episode of *Lewis*, here is your chance to play Whodunnit? Calls on a landline cost £1. On a mobile, could be anything. Here is tonight's prize question:

In this episode of *Lewis*, who is in charge of the investigation? Is it: (a) Inspector Lewis (Kevin Whately)? (b) John Lewis (plc)? (c) Joe Louis?

Lines will remain open until Tuesday week. The number to call is . . .

. . . on this morning's *Today* programme, John Humphrys – the noisy one with a bit of a Welsh accent – was talking to:

(a) Margaret Beckett? (b) Mao Tse-Tung? (c) Rory Bremner?

Ring 0207 580 4468 and ask to be put through to Cash For Questions. You will not be required to hang on for more than 30 minutes. Not many salesmen will call. If you are under ten years old, take the food out of your mouth before speaking, and . . .

. . . thank you, Sian! Now it's the moment all you weather-watchers have eagerly been waiting for, as the lines open for *Umbrella or No Umbrella*. Remember, it could be YOU enjoying a slap-up fish dinner on the Met Office roof with Esther Rantzen if you can correctly answer tonight's teaser. Did the lovely Sian just forecast: (a) Tsunamis light to variable? (b) Sunny spells with the possibility of rain from the east later? (c) Meteorite showers? Ring the number on your screens right now. If you have any special dietary requirements, terms and conditions apply. Remember to put your tick in the Publicity Please box in this week's *Radio Times* if you wish to be famous, and send it to us, enclosing £5 to cover, should you win, our registered reply . . .

. . . which just about wraps up another fabulous *Charlotte Church Show*. Except of course for our big-money phone-in competition, Who Said F*** Tonight? Was it:

(a) Nelson Mandela? (b) The Dalai Lama? (c) Everybody?

The number to call is on the bottom of your screens right now. If numbers are not your thing, you are allowed to ask a smart friend to help, although in those circumstances you may be required to share tonight's star prize, a month in Bangor and a really big cake, worth almost . . .

. . . may just be time for tonight's *News Quiz*. Did Huw say that the missiles were heading for (a) Rockall? (b) South Uzeira? (c) London?

Ring the number on your screen, but do please make it sharpish, and here's a handy clue: if you happen to live in South Uzeira or Rockall, you may well have an outside chance of collecting tonight's . . .

What Did Me In The Holidays

To all the thousands of you reading this in plaster, in traction, and in bitter self-reproach, you have my deepest sympathy. Particularly as you have just come back – or, rather, been brought back – from your first big holiday break of the season. Many of you, indeed, are limping on that break; a lousy pun, I agree, but I shan't be deploying any really classy puns today, since the last thing I want is to have you in more stitches than you already are.

I know all this because I have seen the RoSPA report stating that holiday injuries are increasing exponentially year on year, but only partly because people are annually taking ever more adventurous trips: while it is to be expected that those engaged in whitewater bungee-jumping or carrying an alligator up the north face of the Eiger may encounter a twinge or two, my concern is for the vast majority of holidaymakers who, according to RoSPA, hurt themselves by taking minor exercise to which they are not accustomed and for which they have not prepared.

Since RoSPA therefore advocates basic pre-holiday training, let me offer a few tips. Pack your case a month before you leave, and practice throwing it into the boot of your car every day, so that when your Bulgarian mini-jalopy driver turns up to take you to Heathrow and stares at you while you lug your case out, your shoulder will be up to the task of chucking it on top of his filthy spare wheel. This exercise will also strengthen muscles required later when you have to get your hand-luggage into the overhead locker without cabin crew giggling themselves helpless at the new dent in your head.

You would also be wise to suss out the route to Heathrow. Several per cent of all holiday cardiac arrests occur when a Bulgarian with a conked-out satnav arrives in Slough at the moment your plane is passing overhead.

If you do get there on time, remember that you will have to stand on one leg to take your shoe off for the security joker. Practise this at home for as long as it takes, or risk falling against the thing rolling your jacket through X-ray. Also train yourself to bend, so that, when all your knick-knacks fall out of what has become your full metal jacket and you try to collect them from under the rolling thing where they have themselves rolled, you can stand up again. Flying is painful enough, without doing it on all fours.

You will find that a few months' hearty jogging will prepare you for what happens next, because nothing happens next. Much of your flight will be carried out on foot, since not only is your gate several kilometres away, but, *pace* Omar Khayyam, the moving walkway, having quit, moves not. And do be sure your marathon training was conducted while towing a wheeled bag under total control: a holiday wound is bad enough when you sustain it, but when someone else sustains it through your culpable ineptitude, an arm and a leg could cost you an arm and a leg. Because there's no such thing as a good trip.

Wrist Assessment

OH, look at you, snuggled like a dormouse into a wobbling nest of twinkly Hodgson & Burnett wrapping paper torn off all your lovely presents; your new Smythson's cream-laid notepad, hand-pulped from sustainable bing-bong trees by Samoan lovelies on your knee (the pad, not the lovelies), your new Gabassori Maestro fountain-pen fat and fluent in your grateful fingers, writing your Christmas thank-you letters.

What a very good dormouse you are, to be writing so swiftly to all your hugely generous and irreproachably stylish donors! But, look again, is that not a furrow wrinkling your brow as you struggle to compose a suitable response to your extraordinarily bountiful Aunt Jocasta? You are thinking: Stone me, the last thing I wanted was a bloody Patek Philippe Calatrava! The old dear has forked out £24,000 for a solid gold albatross; it is not only around my wrist, it is around my neck.

And goose-flesh rises on that neck now, as you suddenly sense that, while you were glancing at your wondrous new watch, someone was glancing at you. You turn your head quickly, just in time to spot your 12-year-old son retreating from the doorway behind, and you realise that he might well have seen the same advert his Great Aunt Jocasta saw. The kid has clocked the slogan: 'You never actually own a Patek Philippe. You merely look after it for the next generation.'

Funny beggars, the Swiss: a unique mix of horology and cupidity, which, in Patek Philippe's Geneva bunker, has hit its apogee; but, typically, without an instant's reflection on the human consequences. How truly unsavoury the notion is that everything you own must perforce be a canny investment – do not put your money in rosebuds while ye may, do not come and kiss me, sweet and twenty, it's diamonds that are forever. Why not tattoo your Grossanlegerbank account number on your left buttock to enable, should you suddenly clog-pop, your heirs and assigns to become our new clients as soon as possible?

Oh, look yet again, the next generation has come into the room to ask if he may have a shufti at Daddy's new watch. Is there a hint of Midwich Cuckoo in his covetous eyes? Do you perhaps hear the turn of the screw? Could the little chap be calculating which of your less desirable assets he might one day have to flog in order to pay the Chancellor's £9,600 cut of his inherited Calatrava? Worse yet, will you ever again be able to stand beside him on a railway platform with the old confidence, or drink the solicitous cocoa he has brought to your bedside, let alone show him how to load the Holland & Holland 12-bore over-and-under for which you were just about to write and thank your dearest chum at Goldman Sachs?

Think about it, dormouse, right now. There is no present like the time.

Any Old Iron

DID you see the *Daily Mail* photograph of Ginette Pike? She was drying her hair. Big news? Yes, for the *Mail*: what she was doing it with was a 40-year-old dryer inherited from her grannie. Could be a record, apparently, so the paper invited any readers still using even older domestic appliances to write in. *The Times* missed out on this big story, but it doesn't matter: *The Times*. doesn't need readers to write in. It's got me.

Miss Pyke has opened a can of worms, especially for anyone who got married a good three years before her hairdryer was even a twinkle in her grannie's eye. I don't know what she opened it with, but I bet it wasn't a 43-year-old wall-mounted electric can opener. Certainly not one that has been wall-remounted six times, as you can see from the Polyfilled holes in the wall it is mounted on. Mrs Coren and I still use this wedding present, when we want to open a tin which falls *off* the can opener as soon as the tin has been half opened, because, after 43 loyal years, its magnet is poignantly feeble. No matter, we have trained ourselves to catch it as it falls, just an inch or so before it hits the Kenwood food mixer which stand beneath it.

The Kenwood is the same age, and we love it. I know when Mrs Coren is making a cake even when I am working four floors above, because the bowl is dented and the mixing-hook wonky, and I find that the rhythmic clunking interrupts my work hardly at all. The cakes turn out very well, too. 'How's the sponge?' Mrs Coren will ask. 'Wonderfully lumpy,' I reply. 'Just the way I like it.'

The mixer came, of course, with a blender. We can still get the blender to fit on top of it with only the smallest of hammers. That the stopper which fits almost totally into the lid has to be held on while the blades are whirling is a great boon: to tell whether any more seasoning is required, you simply lick the soup out of your palm.

And just look at the kitchen telephone. It has a dial. It was in the house when we bought it, and we both cried: 'Retro!' as soon as we saw it, for that is the kind of people we are. We love using it: dialling introduces a soothing deceleration to the hectic times we live in, and the inevitable misdialling with soupy fingers is even better: you meet so many interesting new people. It is also, of course, attached to the wall by a plaited cord, so cannot be snatched by villains. They would have to pull the whole house after them.

And my own hairdryer? Bought in Oxford a full ten years before Ginette's grannie dug into her purse, it ran very hot, vital for a full head of hair. But that it now runs barely lukewarm no longer matters: indeed, as the globe boils up, cooling a hairless dome will be essential in the sultry days ahead.

Now, shall we re-descend to the kitchen? I have something fabulous to show you. These seven toasters give us endless hours of . . .

*Good G*lly!*

THOSE of you reading this propped against the teapot – this, not you – may find some of its words obscured by sticky blobs. That can happen to books. It may, though, not happen for very much longer. The marmalade industry is dying. The future is not bright. It is not orange.

The reason, claimed a spokesperson, is that children no longer like marmalade, and discourage their parents from buying it. Nothing could be further from the truth; but that is where the truth has been banished, because the spokesperson couldn't speak it. Had he spoken it, a certain word would have been inescapably involved, and people would have come round to the spokesperson's house and sprayed nasty things on it.

For the truth is that children never liked marmalade, but encouraged their parents to buy it. At least, they encouraged them to buy the top-sellers, Robertson's Golden Shred and Silver Shred, because of what the jars had on their labels. And here comes the word, albeit in a form designed to appease those who would otherwise reach for their aerosols and run straight round to *The Times*: what the jars had on their labels were g*ll*w*gs. They could be cut out by children who, when they had collected five of them, would send them off to Robertson's and get back an enamel g*ll*w*g brooch.

There was a huge variety of enamel g*ll*w*gs. I myself had three: one held a cricket bat, one held a rifle, and one, dear God, actually held a banjo. I was quite young at the time, mind, as people of my age tended to be 60 years ago, and I pinned all three g*ll*w*gs on my Osidge Primary School blazer lapel, which is what people of my age did. David Collingwood had five, and when the rest of us saw him coming, we stepped aside. Respect meant something rather different, back then.

But none of us liked marmalade; we just forced it down pluckily, or threw the jars away when our mums weren't looking, or, like Michael Ibbotson in 4a, shoplifted it from the Co-op, just for the labels. Robertson's had struck a gold, and silver, seam. Until, of course, consciousness changed.

I have never fully understood why it did, because the g*ll*w*g was the best-loved stuffed toy ever. It may, I suppose, have been something to do with the last syllable, but you would be wrong to castigate it as w*g, since the word was invented in 1895 by an American author called Upton, who conflated it from God and pollywog. A pollywog is a tadpole. You know what God is. And together, they can't half sell jamjars.

But if, to save moribund marmalade, it is too late to bring the g*ll*w*g back, I see no reason why producers shouldn't come up with new cross-culturally inclusive alternatives: little rabbis blowing bagpipes, say, little imams scaling maypoles, little fakirs chucking boomerangs, little popes on tricycles, and whatever else takes this or that sectarian fancy.

There should even be room for little ballerinas waving swastikas.

Manifold Pressures

FIFTY years ago this week, I raised my hand to ask Mr Milward if I might be excused, I walked out of the classroom, I put on my school cap, and I took the 29 bus to my appointment with the most important man in the world. And there he was, sitting in a bottle-green Austin A35. Not in the driving seat, of course, because that was where I was going to sit; so I did, and I checked the mirror and I started the engine and I drove off behind a flappy L-plate; and when I drove back, half an hour later, the most important man in the world took off the L-plate and shook my hand.

How literal can a rite of passage get? Nor had it made me merely a man; it had made me a free one, with a free world, palpably, at my feet: bliss was it in that dawn to be alive, but to have three pedals was very heaven. I could go anywhere, much of the anywhere at any speed, and no one would know where I or the anywhere was, and when I got to it, I could park anywhere in it, free. And not only could I drive any old car to do this in, I could drive every old car, there being no MOT test, so I bought a Morris 10/4 much older than I was, not because of pubescent yearning for a mature partner, but because she was anybody's for a tenner.

Love is not love which alters when it alteration finds, eh? Let me turn from my keyboard now, half a century on, and stare at the car below my window. Though she is much younger than I am, and cost rather more than a tenner, under the window is where she spends 99 per cent of her time. If I drive her half a mile south to buy a paper, it will cost me £8 for congestive affrontery, plus £50 for not galloping back the further half-mile I had to drive to the only £5 parking meter I could find faster than the three Westminster sprinters who are racing me to her. The record of all this activity will be held at CCTV House, so that the Chief Constable will know where I have been, and how, and why, and also be able gleefully to pass the DVD on to the Department for Jailing People Who Fasten Their Seatbelts After Moving Off.

If rage-fuelled incaution makes me drive my £63 newspaper home at 30.1 mph, worse may happen: road humps may dislodge my bridgework, a MET helicopter report me for whizzing past Regent's Park mosque in a manner likely to unnerve armed response units secreted in the shrubbery, and a beak fine me £500 and shred my licence. Probably on the day my car is clamped outside my dentist's surgery. Or towed away from it.

Do not ask if I ever drive out of London to go and live in a motorway jam, rather ask how happy I am to contribute to the £62 billion required to set up a pay-as-you-go system for the mugs who do. And since, in my 50 years of driving to the Moon and back, things only ever got worse, how long can it be before just staring at the car below my window brings an ASBO to my mat?

I sometimes wonder whether, if Mr Milward had said in 1957 that I couldn't be excused, I wouldn't be a happier man today.

Chinese Puzzle

OH, really, Secretary of State? Mandarin, you say? Can you say it in Mandarin? Ah. Nevertheless, you, as Education Education Education Secretary, have cheerily expressed your expectation that, by 2012, when the Chinese athletes arrive at the Olympic Village, lots of Britons will be able to chat with them. Asked the way to the nearest Nandrilone r Us, our children will be in a position to give detailed directions, without pointing.

Urn. Do you know how many teachers of French there are in Britain? Yes, you do, because I have just phoned your Department, and they know, so I know that you know. There are 23,000. Teachers of Mandarin? 78. Something of a task ahead, then, if pupils are to drop French in favour of Mandarin: you will have to find 22,922 Mandarin beaks pretty sharpish.

But first things first, because that is the way education works. Of the 200,000 children soon to take GCSE French, do you know how many will end up able to chat to French people in it? 12. Only an educated guess, I admit – guesswork was my core curriculum – but I spend a lot of time in France, where I see a lot of Britons, most of them middle class and therefore middle-educated in French, and do you know what I see them doing? Shouting and gesticulating. They are not doing it to pass themselves off as French, they are doing it because they can't. If they need something for the weekend, the only word the shopkeeper will recognise is weekend; he will have to rely on sign language to work out what the something is.

I do not know why, when their own language is so complicated, Britons find simpler languages impossible, but has it not struck the Education Secretary that Mandarin might prove a little tricky? To start with the alphabet, you can't: there isn't one. Where you start is with the first of 50 thousand different characters. Since each can be pronounced in four different ways to articulate four different meanings, we arrive once more at the figure of 200,000: in other words, as it were, if each of the pupils currently struggling to learn French were to learn instead one different Mandarin word each by 2012 (a big ask, I promise) they would all have to turn up in the Olympic Village if Britain is – how did the Secretary of State put it? – 'to raise our game, in order to compete in an increasingly globalised economy.'

To which end he has a further vision, some might say one even more Olympian, of Britons flocking by slow boat to China to buy, to sell, to holiday, to settle, doing it all in fluent Mandarin. Oo-er. Given that globetrotting Britons never use any accent but their own, even that extraordinary handful who have managed to learn a few Mandarin words will have been unable to master the requisite ten tones: they will ask the way to the terracotta army, and find themselves ordering double glazing.

Nor is shouting and gesticulating advisable: remember that chap who tried it in Tiananmen Square? They drove a tank over him.

Trick Questions

OH, look, there is a new Home Office initiative. Unless, by the time this book gets to press, the editors will have corrected that to New Home Office initiative; since that is what we might well, by tomorrow, have, given the volatility of events in Marsham Street. (Note to any out-of-touch editors: I am not wrong, Marsham Street is the new address for the old Home Office. The old Home Office moved there last year from Queen Anne's Gate. They did that following a new initiative which declared that the old Home Office was sick and tired of genderist puns about the way one of our beloved sovereigns (1707–1714) found herself walking after 22 pregnancies.

And if you think: thank God, that is today's bit of silliness out of the way, you are mistaken. We have not got to the new New Home Office initiative yet. This is a plan to embed X-ray cameras into the nation's lamp-posts to enable your great Home Secretary to clock terrorists who are carrying bombs in their underwear.

Though I have many doubts about how far this plan carries the nation forward, I have none at all about how far it carries me back. When I was a boy, it was impossible to buy a comic which did not contain an advertisement for X-ray spectacles. It was aimed at boys who hitherto could only dream of having Superman's X-ray eyes, which they felt to be utterly wasted on Superman, because he never used them to look at women, this being incompatible with truth, justice, and the American way. For our part, we felt it to be totally compatible with the British way, just to uncover the truth about women. So we all sent off five-bob postal orders.

What came back were so opaque that not only could you not see things you couldn't previously see, you couldn't see things you previously could. Many of my generation still bear the scars left by pillar boxes. Though not Gerald Finch: he refused to cough up five bob on the grounds that even if the glasses worked, you would only see Brenda Taylor's bones anyway.

What is clear to me today, however, is that John Reid has been thinking about this for 50 years. I do not know for which minutia of economic history he got his PhD, but it wouldn't at all surprise me to learn that it was the commercial structure of the comic book, not only because so many of his policies patently reflect his early reading, but also because you have only to glance at him to realise that he has modelled himself on Desperate Dan.

That he is growing more desperate with every passing day is surely reflected in the new X-ray initiative. God knows what the Home Office will come up with next, though I recall that the Seebackoscope, enabling you to spot any terrorists following you, was a snip at half a crown. But, given fully booked cells and the judiciary's enmity towards Dr Reid, how will terrorists be punished? Sentenced to a sprinkling of itching powder, probably.

Animal Crackers

*R*EADING *at the weekend that the railings around London Zoo were too low to keep in any animals which escaped from their cages, I was of course thrilled. Because I immediately conflated this news with thoughts of mink, parakeets, and global warming, to arrive at the exciting conclusion that when, any minute now, the Zoo's inmates become outmates, Derwent May's captivating Nature Notes for The Times will probably read somewhat differently . . .*

As the days of spring grow ever balmier, many of you will wake to the unmistakeable sound of your bedroom windows being licked. Slowly drawing back the curtains to avoid startling, you will find yourself eye to eye with a large head. You will be able to identify the animal by its distinct orange markings and the fact that you sleep on the third floor. It is a giraffe. It will almost certainly have another giraffe standing beside it, for this is the season when they are searching for somewhere to mate. My advice is to tiptoe downstairs and move the car to a safe place.

Now is the time when, in Tescos all across the land, you may expect to see short ginger customers jumping up and down in the six-items-or-less queues. Orangutans are impatient creatures, who, should the checkout lady summon a supervisor to query the correct accounting of a bunch of bananas half-eaten en route to the till, may begin throwing trolleys. It is wise not to remonstrate, lest the customer turn his attention to throwing you.

As the hedgerows commence their lush seasonal burgeoning, be especially cautious when plucking wild flowers therefrom. The sinuous tendril you gently ease aside may well be a black mamba, that spry little chappie whose clever camouflage is not his only fascinating feature: the venom of one particularly feisty example is recorded as having once accounted for an entire platoon of Gurkhas, much to the relief of a beleagured Japanese gun crew who had been about to chuck themselves on their own bayonets.

Similarly, with the trout season happily upon us, take particular care when casting for the plump speckled fellow lurking beside a floating log. The log could be out of there in a trice and have your leg off before you know it.

On a closing note, many readers have e-mailed me to express fears that our domestic cats may be threatened by all the ocelots, lynxes, servals and so forth which have escaped into the wild, and enthusiastically bred (an Uxbridge gentleman has written to say that the nocturnal racket has made his wife stone deaf in one ear). The answer is, I'm afraid, that not only will some of our British cats be killed, but also that others may be, how shall I put it, compromised. If you find that your own dear tabby has given birth to kittens able to slice open a tin of Whiskas with a single swipe of their claw, I urge you to seek professional advice at your earliest convenience.

Plug Ugly

JUNE 6. No coincidence there, then. But I am writing this on D-Day minus 1: I do not know what tomorrow will bring. I know what it is supposed to be bringing. I have been anticipating it for a very long time, the planning has been meticulous, the preparation exemplary; and yet, once what tomorrow is bringing is brought, who can guess what it will bring with it? Planning and preparation can go only so far. That is how it is with D-days.

I have known for months that June 6 would be Delivery Day. Mrs Coren has it in writing. That is because it was all Mrs Coren's idea. She wants the world to be a better place. Especially for her, which is why she spent so much time and effort and money on getting the box fitted to our front wall. And the thing inside the box. The thing has to be inside a box, and the box has to have a lock on it, because you have to stop people stealing what is coming into the thing. For the thing inside the box is a plug, and what is coming into it is electricity.

Why would people want to steal the Corens' electricity? To run their electric car. If the plug were not inside a locked box, when our electric car is not plugged into it but pottering about on the electricity from which it is now unplugged, anyone could come along and plug their own car in. Hang on, you say, you have not got an electric car. Wrong: it is being delivered on June 6. By the time you read this, Mrs Coren will have plugged it in, and I shall be staring at it.

I know what I shall see. Go to www.goinggreen.co.uk and you can see it, too. It is called a G-Wiz. That there is something of the cartoon about its name doesn't stop there. Noddy would love it: otherwise indistinguishable from his, this one has a roof. Mrs Coren tells me it will save congestion charges, parking meter fees, petrol costs, insurance payments, road tax, and the planet. In that order. She tells me this while I am staring at it.

When a man says something is all his wife's idea, you may be sure that when you look into his eyes, they will tell you that when he says all, all is what he means. Not that this is the worst idea he has ever heard, only that he thinks it is. I have been driving cars for 50 years. All of them have been quick, all of them have been ragtops, most of them have been red. If I look down from my attic window now, I can see the last of the line. I am lucky enough to live in a house with great views, but the greatest is the one I am looking at right this minute. I shall not be able to look at it for long. On June 6, it will be delivered to someone else, to make way for what is delivered to me. I shall be looking at a toy with a top speed of 40 mph and a range of 40 miles. Today, I am Nuvolari, I am Fangio, I am Schumacher; but tomorrow I shall be Noddy. If I leap in and give it all the wellie there is, after an hour I shall have to knock on someone's door to ask if I can use their plug.

Unfit For Purpose

In a bid to curb binge drinking, the British Beer and Pub Association is to abolish happy hour.

The small man set down the two pints on the table. The table wobbled.

'It's gone on me leg,' said the tall man. He took out a handkerchief.

'I wouldn't do that,' said the small man. 'You'll smell on the bus. Worse if you have to blow your wossname. There may be pregnant women. They will complain the alcohol will affect the size of their baby. You will get thrown off. Arrested, possibly. My advice is to brush it off with your hand.'

'It's stained me trainers now,' said the tall man, 'you silly sod.'

'That's the trouble with trainers,' said his friend. 'We used to have proper shoes. You could widdle with impunity. Don't talk to me about canvas.'

'I widdle a lot more, these days,' said the tall man.

'Have you seen anyone about it?'

'I have been on the waiting list,' said the tall man, 'since 1998.'

'I told him not to fill the glasses right up. I can remember when this pub used to leave a good half-inch at the top. I can remember complaining about it.' He took a sip. 'But at least it used to taste like beer.'

'EU regulations,' said the tall man. 'Brussels has specified that chemical rubbish has to be added to British draft bitter, to protect bottled Belgian. I presume that is also why you did not buy any pork scratchings, due to where they now have to come from more than one country of origin.'

'You wouldn't want to eat anything a Polish pig scratched off,' said the small man. 'I thought about a pickled egg, though.'

'But then you thought, bird flu, am I right?'

'You are not wrong. I have eaten my last Chinese. Also Indian. They put cancer in to colour the sauce.' He lit a cigarette. 'What with catching diabetes off of hamburgers, that only leaves fish and chips.'

'Not for long,' said the tall man. 'There's only three cod left in the sea, and not more than half a dozen haddock. Do not even think about halibut. Any day now, we shall all be eating jellyfish.'

'Provided we can stop it wobbling out of the packet on the way home.'

'I'd eat it there if I were you,' said the tall man. 'You wouldn't want to walk home and get your jellyfish took off you by a mob of hoodies. Also shot, in all probability.'

'By a girl,' said his friend. 'Most violent crime is now committed by infant females. They are the ones who can afford guns, due to maternity benefit. Funny, they would be the first to start yelling if you pulled your handkerchief out on the bus, if they lost the baby they could never afford ammunition.'

'I blame the North Koreans' said the tall man. 'If I was twelve, I'd want it all now, too, before an H-bomb fell on me. Or,' he added, 'an asteroid.'

'Is that for definite?'

'August 3, 2046. As agreed by all known scientists, nem con.'

'Bloody hell, that is the day before my 90th birthday! I

shall never draw my pension. I have worked it out and it could be as much as £4 a week.'

The tall man shrugged. 'You lose some, you lose some. My wife rang me one day last month and said her lottery number had come up. So I went out and bought a new Rover. When I got home she said the prize was a tenner.' He cracked a knuckle. 'And there were 60 of 'em in the syndicate.'

'I don't know where any of us would be,' said the small man, 'if house prices hadn't rocketed.'

'We'll soon find out,' said the tall man. 'According to reliable sources close to everybody who knows anything, we shall all be in negative equity by Christmas. I wouldn't care, but I just spent a ton of money on a major roof extension for the wife's mother. Next thing I know, it's only gone and slid off the roof, hasn't it? Bloody cowboys!'

'Was she in it?' enquired the small man.

'Don't make me laugh.'

'Thinking of which,' said the small man, 'I turned on the radio yesterday morning while I was shaving, the way I always do, and instead of John Humphrys, it was Nicholas Parsons.'

'Tell me about it,' said the tall man. 'I couldn't finish my egg.'

'Still, *Today* was back this morning.'

The tall man drained his glass, and stood up. 'Not before time,' he said.

A Little Touch Of Harry

HERE are a few statistics about J. K. Rowling you may not yet have read.

1. If all the published copies, hardback and paperback, in all translations, of the six Harry Potter books were laid flat, edge to edge, they would entirely cover Brazil.

2. If, however, the Brazilian rainforest continued to be reduced at the current rate, by the afternoon of April 17, 2057 there would be room only for a single-volume tower of all the published copies of the, by then, seven Harry Potter books. It would be 48,977 miles high. It would be the only pile of books visible from Mars.

3. Had, on May 16 last, J. K. Rowling put all her income from the five published Harry Potter books on Archer's Folly in the 3.15 at Haydock Park, which came in by a short head at 100-1, she would have become richer than Bill Gates by £135.84. If, though, she had waited until this week's publication of the sixth book and put all her accumulated money on Jiminy Cricket in the 2.45 at Sandown, she would now be in a position to buy North Dakota.

4. The combined weight of all the six Harry Potter hardbacks, in all translations, is 143 tonnes heavier than Mount Snowdon. Were this to be added to the combined weight of all the six Harry Potter paperbacks, it would be 61 tonnes heavier than Ben Nevis.

5. Of all the children, worldwide, who have bought a Harry Potter, only 32 per cent know it is a book. The largest category of those who think it is something else is the 27 per cent who think it is a box of tissues which opens at the side. The smallest category of those who think it is something else is the 0.0001 per cent located in an exclusive South Kensington finishing school, who believe it to be a deportment aid.

6. Were all the semi-colons in all the Harry Potter books, in all translations, to be typed out in a straight line, they would circle the world twice. Bear in mind that there are no semi-colons in Arabic, Hebrew, Chinese, Japanese, Urdu or Inuit.

7. If all cigarette manufacture suddenly stopped in China, and the 73 per cent of the population who smoked managed to get their hands on all the Harry Potter books ever published, in all translations, they would have enough paper to make themselves 20 roll-ups a day for the next 289 years.

8. The quantity of adhesive used to secure all the pages of the six Harry Potter volumes to their bindings would be enough to cover Wales in linoleum floor tiles.

9. Were the President of the United States ever to yield to pressure from fundamentalist Christian objectors and order every copy of Harry Potter to be burned, global warming would increase by 2.7 per cent. Even on the most optimistic estimate, this would leave only the top 18.7 metres of the Blackpool Tower visible.

10. However, if, in the (admittedly unlikely) event of the President of the United States having signed up to the Kyoto Protocols, the books were not burned but pulped, enough material would be produced to rebuild Falluja entirely in papier-mâché.

11. If each copy of every Harry Potter book published consisted of words different from those in every other copy, it is statistically more than likely that one of the books could have been typed by a chimpanzee.

12. In a recent attempt by a team of mathematicians in Istanbul to work out how much J. K. Rowling had earned in Turkish lire (at 2,318.9 to the £), the university computer blew out all windows within a diameter of 300 metres.

13. You do not have to share J. K. Rowling's passion for necromancy to be troubled by the number 13. All you have to share is common superstition. For if all the copies of Harry Potter ever sold were to be placed in piles of 13 around the world, the statistical likelihood of anyone walking past one of them subsequently falling through an open manhole beggars belief.

NB. All these statistics are taken from an advance copy of *The Guinness Book of J. K. Rowling,* to be published at midnight on July 31st. Those wishing to begin queuing outside bookshops now are advised to seek tickets for places at almost any website you can shake a broomstick at.

Bang To Rights

OH, to be in England – and the moment I stepped off Monday's plane after four homesick weeks, I knew just why. So it is no accident that I launch the first farrago of my autumn term with that hoary *cri de coeur*, since it was the uproarious stand-up Hermann Goering who, when he heard the word culture, reached for his Browning, and his plucky Luftwaffe will shine brightly in what follows – along with the royal family, Enid Blyton, Claridge's, the broad sunlit Cotswolds, the *News of the World*, and Cadbury's Fruit & Nut, and you cannot get more cultural than that.

All this, because the first thing I did at Heathrow was buy *The Times*. It held two glorious stories. The first concerned MI5's revelation of the cunning 1940 plan by some Nazi Baldrick to parachute saboteurs into rationed Britain, who would distribute chocolate bars and tinned plums and fizzy drinks to the salivating war-deprived. The joyful beneficiaries would then scuttle off to gobble their covert goodies, and a few seconds later, blow themselves to bits, for the goodies the baddies had slipped them were bombs: you snapped the chocolate, opened the tin, unscrewed the bottle, and went bang.

Can it be mere coincidence that these were the days of Enid Blyton's pomp? I think not. I think the Abwehr, Teutonically meticulous as ever in their research, believed that in her they had discovered, quite literally, Britain's soft underbelly. Tinned plums, chocolate, lashings of ginger beer? What is this if not *Five Go Off To Blitzkrieg*? The fact that not one booby trap worked is only further proof: for you and I know, though Jerry somehow failed to clock, that a nano second before any human was fragged, Timmy the Dog's keen nose would have told him to bark a monitory 'Arf Arf!'.

And then I turned the page, to the second story. This also involved bibs, tuckers and the Third Reich. Some time ago, Princess Michael of Kent had sat down to a Gordon Ramsey corker at Claridges in the rapt company of a billionaire sheikh, because, though her Gloucestershire bolt-hole Nether Lypiatt was up for sale, it had not attracted much interest until the bloke in the sheet fronted up on its doorstep and began talking serious money. And, on their follow-up date, not only money: for, despite all the Michelin-starred stuff being noisily hoovered up through the nosebags, Mazher Mahmood still managed to persuade the mouth of the radiant vendor opposite to expound all manner of fascinating stuff about the royal family, inside dope (if she will pardon the expression) which, it appears, she had been fatally beguiled into imagining might be a useful part of her sales pitch. Not so. She had been conned. Her lunch date did not make his money by digging up oil, he made it by digging up dirt. He had been parachuted in by The *News of the World* with a smarter booby-trap than tinned plums.

Now, my heart goes out to the Princess. She and I have been quite close, and I once took her to see the most erotic statue in London – it is, since I sense a raised eyebrow, of Sir Arthur Sullivan, and it may be viewed opposite the Embankment entrance to the Savoy, for those of you who are, as it were, curious – and her response was so earthy a giggle that grown men within a radius of perhaps 50 yards went off for a bit of a lie down. So it is not to compound her current embarrassment but to attempt to alleviate it that I remind you that, during the recent misunderstanding between her two countries, her father was a mounted SS officer. It is therefore not beyond the bounds of imagination to wonder whether – in, say, 1940 – he and his trusty horse might not have been parachuted into Britain with a saddlebagful of exploding Fruit & Nut.

We now know that none of the bars went off. So it is not impossible that, in some attic of Nether Lypiatt, there is a brass-bound diddy-box of inherited mementoes containing, among the monocles and armbands and Lugers and cigarette-holders, a bar of chocolate, pristine in its cleverly forged Cadbury's wrapper. Now, do those of us who still respect life's social decencies not relish the idea of the Princess ringing up Mr Mahmood and inviting him down to let bygones be bygones, and, upon his departure, giving him a little snack for his homeward journey? I see her standing at a tall window, drawing aside a velvet swag the better to watch her tormentor stroll down the long drive, pause to snap off a nutty chunk, and blow his head all over Gloucestershire.

Advertisements For Myself

I WAS a lavatory, once. And a pretty convincing one, too, though I say it myself. Indeed, it was saying it myself that, eventually, made me convincing: what I had to say myself was 'Watch out, germs! Here comes Harpic!', and I had to say it over and over again, hundreds of times, until, as the long day's sun sank below the wonky jalousie of my tiny Soho studio, I finally became the most convincing lavatory you ever heard. Truly bog standard.

I don't know, mind, if you did ever hear it. You would have to have been watching afternoon ITV, when those who constitute the target market for domestic hygiene take a short breathless break from mop and aerosol, plonk down before the box with mug and Hobnob, and are brainwashed into disinfectant seduction. You would not, of course, have seen me on that box: you would have seen only a cartoon khazi, the chirpy mouth on its twinkling upturned lid synchronised to my six mesmeric words.

It was, sometime in the early '80s, my big acting break. Sadly, the break itself broke a few ads later, after my voice-over roles as a dancing onion, a time-shared Spanish hovel, and a recently shrunken haemorrhoid unaccountably failed to convince any new advertising agents or their clients that I was irresistible commercial timber. Or, rather, timbre. I did a few auditions, was assured I would be let know, but never heard anything; except Richard Briers or Martin Jarvis or, on one particularly hurtful occasion, Sue Pollard, brilliantly playing what I had pitiably come to think of as my patio door, my egg-whisk, my cat meat.

Which is why, instead of lolling on a burnished Bermudan poop guzzling pâté de foie gras and Dom Perignon from a couple of Asprey buckets while I wait for my helicopter to return with Cameron Diaz, I am still up here in the Camden loft, punching a keyboard. However, if you now direct your glance to the top of this column, you may well share my view that things could very soon take a swift turn for the better. That is because you read in last Wednesday's *Times* that 'drinks companies have been ordered to hire paunchy balding men for advertisements to meet new rules forbidding any link between women's drinking and sex.'

What has ordered the companies to do this is the Committee of Advertising Practice, which, exercised over female binge-boozing, is concerned that current ads showing Brad Pitt and Vinnie Jones supping Heineken and Bacardi respectively – even as George Clooney's pen squiggles a £2.5 million Martini contract – will persuade young women that, were they to front up at the Rat & Cockle in good working order, they could reasonably expect much more than mere pints to be pulled.

I have to say, despite the risk to what have suddenly become my great expectations, that I find the CAP's argument a mite tricky to support. While I know none of these male glamourpusses personally, I cannot but think it highly unlikely that if, sitting quietly at the bar (an even sexier three inches taller as the happy result of the newly stuffed wallet beneath them) these hunks were to be lurchingly approached by a shrieking woman with each mottled eye rolling differentially in her head, above a mouth errantly lipglossed onto her chin and a lava lamp riveted to her tattooed navel, Brad or Vinnie or George would without a second thought fall into her flailing arms simply on the strength of their sharing a fancy for the same tipple.

Nevertheless, I shall go with the flow; and since what is flowing seems to have become unacceptable to the Committee of Advertising Practice, I happily lay before them the tempting stall of my CV and my snapshot. And I do so not solely for the enormous personal gain that their desperate industry will be compelled to front up for the right wrinkly, I also offer myself in the role of caring public altruist, eager to do the state some service. For if these hapless women can be convinced that the only result of sinking a couple of dozen Bacardi breezers and a kegful of pina colada would be to end up with a bald old git whose long-gone best years were spent as a hysterical thunderbox and a talking pile, they might very well sign the pledge tomorrow.

Any day now, I could be seen as the curse of the drinking lasses.

The Rest Is History

OFSTED'S chief inspector of schools, says not only that the history curriculum places far too much emphasis on the Tudors and World War Two, but also that students are unable to remember key dates or major events. If the end-of-term answer paper which just happened to blow into my hands on a capricious Christmas Eve gust is anything to go by, he is not wrong.

1. It was Richard III who got the Tudors started, by losing the Battle of Britain. The poor sod never stood a chance

against the House of Lancaster once it had invented the four-engined bomber. Also, his Scandinavian allies let him down fatally by staying neutral so's they could make ballbearings for both sides: his last words were: 'A Norse! A Norse! My kingdom for a Norse!'

2. The thing Henry VII was most worried about at the beginning of his reign was the Scots. To get James IV of Scotland on side, he sent his illegitimate daughter to marry him. She was a fit-looking woman, though barmy, called Margaret Hess.

3.The person who created the Royal Navy was Henry VIII. One of his really top ideas was the submarine: he made loads of these which hunted in packs under the English Channel and sank all sorts of foreign boats and took jewels and spices and silks off them, but their best result was against the German Armada. Henry's victory was to put Adolf Hitler off the idea of invading England for good. The last Tudor submarine to surface was the *Mary Rose*. My theory about why it didn't come up for four hundred years is that nobody had remembered to tell the captain the war was over.

4. The book *Tudor Cornwall* was written by A. L. Rowse. My teacher, Mr Foskett, who has just done a civil partnership with the Headmaster and is in a bit of a frisky mood, told our class that after A. L. Rowse had finished with *Tudor Cornwall* he went on to do *Stuart Hampshire*. Mr Foskett couldn't stop laughing at this, but none of us could see the joke.

5. In the reign of Henry VIII, the second most important man in England was Cardinal Wolseley. He not only invented the

police-car, he also designed the engine for the Churchill tank. This was to play a major part in the Battle of the Bulge, so called because Henry VIII, who had originally planned to lead the English armoured brigade into battle, made the mistake of having lunch first, and was unable to squeeze himself through the hatch.

6. They are the six wives of Henry VIII. After the fall of London, he took them all up on the roof of his Hampton Court bunker and shot them, to stop the Russians giving them a seeing-to.

7. The Dam Busters raid was led by Wing-Commander Sir Francis Drake, who got the idea for a bouncing bomb during a game of bowls at Plymouth Argyle. The bombs were built by Wallis Simpson, aided by Grommet, but one went off accidently before the raid and killed Drake's dog. I know the dog's name, and would like to get an extra mark for writing it down, but I am not allowed. Can I get an extra mark for saying that Sir David Frost is remaking the film of the raid? I do not know much about the new script, except that when the Lancasters arrive over the Ruhr, Drake chucks open his cockpit window and shouts at the Germans: 'Hallo, good evening, and welcome!'

8. The reasons for her remaining the Virgin Queen were that the only two blokes to get anywhere near were Essex and Raleigh. She turned the first one down because it was better to be called the Virgin Queen than the Essex Queen. She turned the second one down because, although he got rich after inventing the bicycle, he was stingy, and only ever gave her fags or chips, neither of which she could get the hang of. Chips made her cough.

9. The reason the theatre flourished under Queen Elizabeth the First was because it always does when there is a war on. It keeps people's spirits up. The top playwriter was William Shakespeare, the Earl of Bacon, and his theatre was called the Windmill, which never closed. *Hamlet and Cleopatra* was far and away the most popular play put on there, even though Cleopatra had to stand dead still after Hamlet tore all her clothes off. Its best song was 'Whale Meat Again', due to food rationing.

When You And I Were Young, Maggie

SIMON Cellan Jones, director of Channel 4's *The Queen's Sister* admitted to *The Times* that the film 'plays fast and loose with the facts in search of some kind of real truth.' As you would expect, I asked for a transcript of the commentary. Clock these highlights.

On June 6, 1944, Princess Margaret was the first Girl Guide to wade ashore at Normandy. She did not, of course, wade herself; she cantered in on the shoulders of her Brownie-in-Waiting, Joan Collins, under withering cross-talk from the US 4th Division, to her right, and the 2nd British Army, to her left, who were concerned that HRH's Phantom V, bogged down in the sand, was holding up the disembarkation of the Allied armour.

The Princess, however, with what was to become her legendary knack with ordinary people, told a Canadian platoon that if they didn't tow her car onto the road they would all be hanged for treason; so, despite heavy casualties, they did. Her chauffeur, Noel Coward, then drove her towards Caen – where he knew a wonderful little place for lunch – only to be cut off by a squadron of Tigers. Normally more than a match for the statelier Rolls-Royce, the tanks were on this occasion commanded by Oberleutnant 'Binkie' von Ginsberg, who had not only played polo for The Sandringham Tiddleypoms in 1934 but had also enjoyed a brief inter-chukka affair with Mrs Simpson after losing his way to the gents. A chivalrous Junker and coward, he instantly surrendered, for which action the Princess was awarded a Distinguished Service Badge, sewn to her uniform by the little French girl who was to grow into a lively soubrette with interestingly close links to the Royal Family.

In 1955, heartbreak struck when Margaret decided not to marry war hero Mickey Rooney, not because he had been divorced six times, but because she feared that none of their children would be more than four feet tall. But romance returned to her life when, a few years later, she took up with Brian Armstrong-Jones, the fifth Beatle, only to end in tragedy when he was thrown into a swimming-pool, possibly by the Archbishop of Canterbury, for constitutional reasons.

She then began a turbulent affair with her cousin Lawrence Llewellyn Bowes-Lyon, the playboy hill-farmer, to whom she gave huge sums of money in support of his makeover scheme to brew organic gin, which could be poured on Weetabix to create a wholesome yet stimulating breakfast. Sadly, the relationship broke up during one of many experimental tastings, when the couple fell out over whether breakfast should be served with a twist or an olive.

Famously fascinated from infancy by both fancy dress and show business, in 1959 Princess Margaret secretly joined *The Black and White Minstrel Show*. Watched – though not spotted – by nearly 20 million viewers, she sang 'Way Down Upon De Swanee Ribber' so convincingly that it became the anthem of the Weybridge Klavern of the Ku Klux Klan.

By now, her weekend house parties were the talk of both the beau monde and the gutter press – the latter, indeed, these being the days of hot-metal typesetting, once running out of asterisks to describe what HRH didn't give for either of them. Her lovable temper, however, was cleverly brought under control on one famous occasion by none other than Lew Hoad. Commanded to join the Princess and her entourage at Bonkers, the Bermuda hideaway of celebrity society cook Mrs Cecil Beeton, the great Wimbledon champion was invited to play a singles match against his hostess. Hoad, serving blindfold with a ping-pong bat, won the first set 6-0 in under two minutes, whereupon his opponent, having given her Tom Collins an enthusiastic suck, stubbed her cigarette out in Hoad's ear and summoned her protection officers.

After they had had a quiet word with Lew, the match resumed and the Australian lost 6-4. This became known as the Princess Margaret set.

There Was A Crooked Man

UP betimes, dawn the colour of a herring's belly, and out to the frosted car. To find a big glossy card beneath the windscreen wiper. Nothing odd about that, you say, every day there is a new BOGOF pizza cobbler, a new once-in-a-lifetime deal on double-glazed grannie-patios, a new ex-SAS Home Office registered 24/7 security platoon, a new crack squad of state-of-the-art cutting-edge drain-rod engineers, a new purveyor of fresh fish daily to the doorsteps of the discerning gentry, a new girl in town, the former Miss Gdansk, silicone-free, own soap, all major credit cards accepted, absolute discretion assured . . . but, this time, it was none of these.

Nor any old pasteboard card, either, but a fine laminated plastic job. On which giant scarlet capitals hollered 'STOP!' Above this ran the explanatory line: 'Vehicle Crime Prevention Notice', and below it, the kicker: 'There Are No Valuables Left In This Vehicle'. Underneath that, the azure logo of the Metropolitan Police and beside it the slogan: 'Safe in the heart of London.' I plucked it out, turned it over, and learned that: 'You have been given this card to keep in your car, as vehicles in this area are being targeted by thieves. Please leave it on your dashboard when leaving the car unattended. Consider leaving your glove box open, so it can be seen to be empty.'

So I stood there for a bit, doing just that. I further considered leaving the boot open, so targeting thieves could see I had not locked the stuff from the open glove box in the boot; leaving the doors open so they could see I had not shoved the stuff from the open glove box under the seats; and leaving the bonnet open, so they could see I had not hidden the stuff from the open glove box beneath the scuttle. You know jemmies.

But what I most considered was not leaving the notice on my dashboard in the first place; for thieves, you may have heard, know a thing or two about dishonesty, and on being told 'There Are No Valuables Left In This Vehicle', tend to respond 'Pull this one, sunshine.' Especially as the first sentence is unsettlingly ambiguous: notwithstanding its having been toiled over by the top brains of Scotland Yard, it could equally mean: 'There Were Once Valuables In This Vehicle But There Are None Left', which strongly suggests that breaking into this car is a doddle. Give us that coat-hanger, Wayne.

I do wish the top brains had come to me. If they had said, 'We have a bit of a problem, Al, more cars than ever are being turned over, but the police can do nothing, they have got their hands full going round poking notices under windscreen wipers, got any ideas?', I would have suggested that drivers be advised to leave a rucksack on the back seat with wires dangling from it, preferably attached to a clock, and a luggage-label reading: 'Osama bin Laden, 13a, Pondicherry Crescent, Ealing.' Either that or gum a luminous sign to the rear window announcing: 'Turkish poultry on board.'

As to their keynote slogan, what possessed the Met to come up with: 'Safe in the heart of London'? For that is exactly what I have, and I see no reason to advertise the fact to villains who, having ransacked my car, seek to take the next step up the acquisition chain. And no, since you ask, I take no comfort from the probability that innovative Old Bill policy is, even as I type, putting together a second elegant plastic notice reading: 'There Are No Valuables Left In This Safe', and advising me to keep its door open.

Still, needs must when the devil drives, and if what he is driving is my car up to my door, its boot considerately left open by me to make it easier for him to heave my safe into it, then I suppose the Met must do everything in its power to stop him, even if it means suspending all police leave in the never-ending battle to deploy plastic notices round the clock before rushing back to the nick to spend the rest of the day squinting at CCTV footage in the desperate hope of clocking someone doing 41 mph on Hammersmith Flyover at 3 a.m.

It is incumbent on each and every one of us to be pro-active in this great new crime initiative. Why not make your own deterrent placards? Before going out for a walk, hang round your neck: 'Do Not Mug This Man, He Is Carrying No Cash, Credit Cards, Cellphone, Or Keys'. Fearful of copping a house-trashing in your absence? Try: 'Do not piss on this garden, we are growing top-quality Colombian Gold, please call later.' Missed the last bus? 'Do Not Attempt To Rape This Woman, He Is A Cabinet Minister In Drag.'

And mind how you go.

Time Check

In all the 31 years, 8 months, 22 days, 13 hours and 27 minutes that I had been writing regularly for *The Times*, I had never been as gobsmacked by anything in it as I was at 8.12 a.m. on Monday, January 16, 2006, the minute up to which all those other minutes had led. In the interests of precision, I wish I could tell you how many seconds there were on the end of the minutes, but I can't. That is because, when the minutes began, back in 1974, I did not have an Artex clock. None of us had. We did not know about the Artex clock until Monday morning, at 8.12, when we opened our copies of *The Times*.

To page 8. Where, beneath two unforgivably sloppy recipes for, on the left, duck salad with tarragon from Thomasina Miers, and, on the right, roast chestnuts from Joanna Weinberg, there was an advertisement from Times Offers Direct which put both these women to professional shame. How Ms Miers will ever hold up her head again after telling her readers to marinate the duck for 'a minimum of one hour, but preferably three to four', or Ms Weinberg go out in public after telling hers, even more slaphappily, to roast the chestnuts until 'one of them pops with a loud bang', I cannot begin to imagine. The sooner each coughs up £19.95 for an Artex clock to bolt beside her hob, the likelier both are to stave off their leaving parties.

For the Artex clock, according to the rubric which so unprecedentedly gobsmacked me, is 'guaranteed to be accurate to less than a second in a million years.' That is one hell of a guarantee. I know it to be an honest one, too, because it carries *The Times* imprimatur, which means that the most nit-picking lawyers in the world – they have a collection of my own nits which is second to none – have nodded it through. They are confident that if, in 1,000,2005 AD, an owner of an Artex clock bangs on the front door of *The Times* and demands his money back on the grounds that, after only 999,999 years, his clock is two seconds fast, he will not have a leg to stand on.

If, that is, he has legs at all. He's a queer cove, your Johnny Evolution, and anything might have happened to *Homo sapiens* by then. Either that, or global ennucleation will have ensured that the only creature left to survive will, by 1,000,2005, have developed into *Cockroach sapiens,* who will have a lot of legs and be able to carry several iffy Artex clocks while still having a couple of legs free to bang on the *Times* door with. Provided, of course, that it is still *The Times* and not *The Daily Cockroach*; in which event the management may well disclaim any obligation to honour the guarantee offered by their predecessor in 2006. Should you wish clarification on this point before ringing 0870 789 0716 to order your clock, I suggest you ring *The Times'* lawyers. If, mind, unable to contain your excitement, you ordered it as soon as you saw Monday's ad, I really don't know what to suggest.

Some of you may not care: you may hold the view that since the clock will by 1,000,2005 no longer be yours but the property of a cockroach to whom you have no genetic connection, that is an end of the matter. Others more optimistic, blindly confident that the human race will not, any day now, vaporize itself, may be mortified at the thought that its distant descendant – let us call it grandchild[786] – will discover that, having been handed down successfully through 30,000 generations, its Artex clock is now on the fritz. Worse yet, your descendant may discover this by a life-changing shock: it could turn up for the first day at its first job, dressed in its smart new outfit, clutching its smart new briefcase, only to hear: 'What time do you call this? You should have been here two seconds ago,' and find itself out on its ear.

This could be even more disastrous: if the human race has not vaporized itself, by 1,000,2005 AD there will be, according to my slide-rule, over two trillion people on the planet. Jobs will therefore be extraordinarily scarce, and employers extraordinarily choosy (hence the punctuality discriminator), so that anyone luckless enough to lose his on the very first day might well have no option but to jump off Westminster Bridge and drown himself. Or rather, given the effect global warming will have had on the River Thames by then, break his neck.

Did I hear you ask if the Artex is an alarm clock? Not half it isn't.

Now We Are Sex

*A*DVISERS *to the Department of Education have advocated compulsory sex instruction in primary schools. A bit late for that, surely?*

daer santa:
this crismas I would like a set of wills, I do not want no ordnry peddle car tho, yu canot pull wiv sunnink ware berds can see your nees going up and down, yu look like a kid, i want wun of them they do with battries, prefbly a harf-skale frarri or lambergini or simlar, also the seets hav to go flat to make a bed, narmean, i do not have to drore pitchers, we are bofe men of the werld, red wuld be favrite, wiv wite hide, yores, darren

dear satna:
i have been best mates wiv david pirkins from 4 dores up sinse we was 9, munce and munce now, we get on rill wicked, i hav shown him mine and he hav shown me his, and i have just read on the bottem of the parot's cage that it is now posble for 2 yung men to marry wich meens i wuld get harf-shares in his gameboy and ipod and singed rio ferdnand shert and 2-liter flaggen of sir clif richard fragranse, also if he tragicly fel under a bus i wuld get harf the premian bonns his gran giv him for his crisnin, so wot i wuld like for crismas is a sivil partnership stifficate, i have bin up the post offis for a naplication form and they tole me to pis off. its stil the same ole story, a fite for luv and glory, but i am sure yu hav these things in lapland, it

is orl the rage there, i hav seen my dads swede videos, yores, boris

deer Father Cristmas:
i do not kno if yu are aqucwainted wiv Father Merphy, it is posible you were at Vatican Junior Infants together, but even if yu do not kno him persnly yu both sing from the same wossname and see i to i wen it cums to cherch stuf, so i wunder if yu culd hav a word with him becaus all i wont for cristmas is for him to stop poakin his fat nose in ware it is not wonted, he sez if he catches me one more time in the orgn loft with samanther thingy – i do not know her naim, tall fit girl, brests cummin up a treet and no braces to speek of – he wil blo the wissel on me and i wil not be aloud to be josef in the nativty play, i wil have to be a donky, mi mum wuld kil me, josef is ded eesy, mi mum just chuks a sheet over me and winds a towl round mi hed, but with donkys yu have to sow eers and a tale on, she is rubish at sowing, seesons greetings, adam

dere snata:
i am riting on behalf of my partnr, nicklas, 8, on acount of he wares this micky mouse wotch, and i am ashamed to be seen out wiv him, it is not sheek like yu see in mens magzines, i wuld like him to ware sunnink cool and fashnibble such as a wane roony wotch, wich he wuld do if yu brung him wun for crismas. if yu felt he woznt reddy for that, praps yu culd meet him halfway, with, frinstance, a micky roony wotch. for miself, i wuld like a DVD of teddys bare piknik, yuors, cheryl

dear santer:
hallo, i wuld like a tikkit for a 10-30 singals hollyday in the sun, i hav seen sunnink like that on the telly ware there is

big gerls runnin about wobblin on wite beeches and splashin about in the rollin scurf and leepin up in the air doing vollyball and wen they cum down agane there is a bloak waitin to catch them and they all larf and go off holding hands for a drink with a flower in it, and i wuld like to be one of them bloaks, i wuld hav no problem catchin them provided they wasn't too big, i keep wikkit for the under-13s and can also do 90 pressups, happy crismas, shaun

deer satan:
becos it is yore jobb to keep yore eer to the ground yu wil hav herd that the topp toy this cristmas is the tyco cyber shocker, a snipp at £74.99, wich is a radio-controld ball wich terns into a monstr at the tuch of a butten and runs about doin evrything yu say. i wuld like won wear yu tuch the butten and it terns into jenfer lopez. sharlot cherch wuld do at a pinch, yors, norman

dere santa:
i go to a progresiv school and hav been doing sex education for 3 years since i was 5 and came topp in my theory paper last turm and got a cup and a persnly sined copy of the book that wun this yeer's Bad Sex Award, but wen it cum to the practical, the Hedd rote 'Must try harder' on mi report, so wot i wuld like for crismas is a large jar of Junior Viagrer, thank yu, Eric

Chicken Run

'THERE'S a special providence in the fall of a sparrow. If it be now, 'tis not to come; if it be not to come, it will be now; if it be not now, yet it will come: the readiness is all.'

Spot on, Hamlet, the bird flu situation in a nutshell. Tragically, 130 lines later, he was dead; not, mind, from handling an iffy sparrow, nor even as the result of telling one of Yorick's infinite Danish jests about 72 virgins, but just because the flesh is heir to a thousand natural shocks, and you never know your luck. Which, as you have anticipated, brings me to Dr John Reid.

Quite why it should have been the Defence Secretary to whose lot it fell last Sunday to reassure us with the helpful 'Don't panic!' I find it difficult to guess. But not impossible: evoking – as how could it not – the image of Corporal Jones running about like a, sorry, headless chicken, might it be that it is not Defra at all but the MoD which has hit upon a cunning plan for our protection? In short, given that Tommy Atkins is already overstretched from Basra to the Khyber Pass and thus in no position to be deployed in ack-ack batteries along our eastern seaboard, banging away at anything airborne with a runny beak, does Dr Reid envisage remustering the Home Guard?

I think we should be told. I have things to do, columns to write, shelves to put up, roses to prune, cats to worm, and if, any minute now, someone is going to hammer on my front door, hand me a Lee Enfield, a whistle, a pair of binoculars, and a travel pass to Warminster-on-Sea, I need to put my affairs in order. There is also the question of my rank to be addressed: I do not intend, at my age, to be squarebashed up and down the shingle in blistering war-surplus boots by some stupid boy. I want nothing less than a colonelcy, a Sam Browne belt, a camouflaged Hillman Minx with a fit ATS cracker at the wheel, and, in the event of successfully leading my devoted men against a vastly outnumbering horde of enemy gulls coughing their way ashore at Clacton, a DSO.

There is also Mrs Coren to be considered. She is a busy woman, and cannot be expected to start digging for victory at the drop of a hat. If the government stands poised not only to exterminate all our chickens but also – since nobody seems to know anything about anything – to raise queries about the culinary safety of sheep, cattle and pigs which may have been splattered from the skies with the infected droppings of anything my brave troops have been unable to shoot down, the nation may be forced to subsist on whatever it can grow in its back garden. This is not Mrs Coren's thing: if Dr Reid wants her to get up and go outside with a spade and a packet of seeds, he will have to ban Sudoku first. Then again . . .

. . . sorry to have paused in full flight, but talk of the garden reminded me that we have a wire thing hanging up for tits and I had to run out and bin it. I do not know if British tits could catch anything off French ducks – this may be a foul canard, a joke for which I apologise, but, trust me, it avoided my risking one about tits – but I cannot take that chance. It would be highly irresponsible of me to march off to war leaving peanuts hanging where they could wipe out much of north London.

It's only a small garden, I noticed. It had never before struck me that, once a couple of rows of victorious carrots have been sorted out, there'll hardly be room for an Anderson shelter. Younger readers will have to look that up. Older ones will immediately understand that, when I am away doing my bit, I will be unable to rest easy in my bunk unless I know that Mrs Coren has somewhere to go where falling swans won't get her.

Of course, there's always the outside chance that Uncle Sam will come to our aid. I am old enough to remember that in the Last Lot, while he was waiting to see which way the Battle of Britain went, he sent us powdered egg. It came in yellow wax-papered cartons with an eagle on them, possibly to reassure us that American birds had nothing contagious to be ashamed of. Either that, or it was powdered eagle eggs, you couldn't tell from the taste: many diners, indeed, concluded it must be cement, graciously sent to help us shore up blitzed buildings. But generous, however you look at it, and who knows, Uncle Sam may find it in his roomy heart to help us out again. As our Defence Secretary well knows, he owes us one.

Austen Seven

HAVING read last weekend that 'the Jane Austen craze has now permeated every level of the culture,' I decided to google this observation for myself. Here is a random selection from the 794,000 entries:

United Breweries are delighted to announce that, following extensive theme refurbishment, two of their keynote gastro-pubs have now reopened as The Sense & Whistle, in Notting Hill, and, in Wilmslow, Emma's Head.

Nine days after her husband Ronald fell into the habit of answering her every domestic question with: 'It is a truth universally acknowledged that . . .' West Byfleet dinner-lady Mrs Alice Healey, 57, shot him dead.

Following a frustrating period in the celebrity doldrums, hilarious comedy duo Cannon & Ball have just relaunched themselves as Pride & Prejudice.

The film world is a-buzz with the thrilling news that Working Title is soon to go into production with the screen adaptation of *Jane's Fighting Ships*. The finished script has already been handed to them by the incomparable Andrew Davies, who says that while remaining true in every significant aspect to the spirit of the original book, the screenplay inevitably contains just a few small changes necessitated by the translation to the cinema. Feisty Abbey Northanger, radiant commander of the nuclear submarine

HMS *Persuasion*, will be played by Billie Piper, Russell Brand stars as Sir Woodhouse, her dreary First Sea Lord husband, while the Chinese winkler found miraculously alive in the belly of a giant squid tragically dismembered by friendly nuking – the man for whom Cap'n Abbey irresistibly falls after he is winched dripping from the freezing Aral Sea – is to be portrayed by Colin Firth.

Following their board's unanimous decision, Division Two stalwarts Mansfield Town are henceforth to play as Mansfield Park. Ecstatic manager Billy Dearden told Monday's press conference: 'We are over the wossname. This is the result we came for.' Asked whether the rebranding would affect their relations with arch-rivals Chesterfield, Mr Dearden declared: 'For what do we live but to make sport for our neighbours, and laugh at them in our turn?'

Challenged 18 times by Jeremy Paxton over the new caring Conservative Party policy document, 'Sensibility', Mr David Cameron finally admitted he hadn't actually read it, but he was determined to take it on holiday with him.

Rung up by one of his most senior wags to enquire whether this would do, or would even more examples be required, the Editor of Mr Rupert Murdoch's fashionably retitled flagship, *The Prejudice*, told Mr Coren: 'You have delighted us long enough.'

Any God Will Do

FOLLOWING reports that the threatened dismemberment of the Church of England over the issue of homosexual prelates is apparently persuading hordes of disaffected Anglicans to up sticks and defect to Roman Catholicism, fretting thousands of you have, not surprisingly, written to ask me for my expert guidance in this perplexing matter.

'All right,' you tell me, 'we have seen the writing on the wall, any minute now we will find ourselves going into church of a Sunday morning and forced to listen to sermons about making our lives over, starting with the bedroom curtains, and parables involving Shirley Bassey or Judy Garland, also singing 'Abide With Me' to the tune of 'Candle in the Wind'; not for us, thank you, but we do not want to become Roman Catholics either, all that confession stuff, you never know who's behind the grille, it could well be some undercover ratbag from the *Daily Mirror*, plus incense all over your best suit and wafers not being allowed on the Atkins diet, and never certain where you are when it comes to how's your father, or should I say how's your Father, ha-ha-ha, so are there any other religions you can suggest which might do it for me? I am not what you'd call religious exactly, but it's always useful to have something to put on the form when applying for a road fund licence and so forth.'

A very tricky one this, since I clearly do not have the space here to go into any great detail, but knowing the British people as I do, I think I may at least be able to come up with a few helpful pointers for those in what we major theologians call doubt.

Judaism, for example, has considerable appeal. The soup is good, and you can keep your hat on indoors, thereby making a considerable saving on fuel costs. Also, since you will not be allowed to drive on Saturdays, your car will last about 14 per cent longer than gentile ones. Furthermore, books are read back to front, which means that you do not have to plough through the whole of the new Jeffrey Archer to find out what happens.

Islam, however, may suit you even better, in that if you don't want to read the new Jeffrey Archer at all, you can not only publicly burn it, you can apply to have him shot. The main drawback with Islam is that you will have to take your shoes off upon entering the mosque. If it is a big mosque, it may take you all day to find them again.

Buddhism is terrific if you are bald. Nobody will ever know. You can also spend all day walking up and down Oxford Street without ever having to buy anything, and with no socks to wash when you get home. Moreover, the principle of reincarnation is immensely attractive: you could come back as Bill Gates or George Clooney. But then again, you could come back as Jeffrey Archer.

Sikhism, on the other hand, is terrific if you are not bald. Being prohibited from cutting your hair or shaving means that you will never have to visit a barber. You will thus never have to sit in a chair while someone asks you if have read the latest Jeffrey Archer yet, and – whatever your answer – spends the next fifteen minutes retelling it.

Taking on Hinduism, though, would involve you in a somewhat more complex decision process, fraught as the religion is with a multitude of pros and cons. To take only one example, while you do not have to find your own wife, which saves you a fortune in flowers, perfume, and chocolates, you have to keep the shop open until midnight, all week, because you never know when a non-Hindu in search of a wife might want to buy flowers, perfume, or chocolates. You may also have to stock the new Jeffrey Archer: since this will almost certainly be on a sale or return basis, with mobs of customers coming and going at an unsettling rate, the accountant in your family may well be compelled to stay up far later than his primary school-teacher recommends.

Shinto would be, in every sense, the simplest choice. You get to fold your own house for no more than the cost of the old newspapers involved, you do not need to cook your food, you are never required to clap more than one hand, and the Japanese translation of the new Jeffrey Archer will be in the form of a haiku of only seventeen syllables.

So there you have it. Good luck, ex-Anglicans, and God, whichever One you choose, bless you. But if none of the above appeals to you, remember that the Mormons are always on the lookout for new recruits. They're a really nice crowd, with only one major drawback: you have to wear a shiny blue suit and a permanent grin and tell everybody you meet about this truly wonderful book of yours. You will thus run the constant risk of being mistaken for Jeffrey Archer.

How Heavy Is That Doggie In The Window?

IF you are a dog-lover, the Chartered Society of Physiotherapy has a bone to pick with you: you love your dog so much that you have stopped picking bones for it. Instead, you are picking biccies and choccies and munchies and chewies, which are turning your doggies into fatties, especially as you are no longer taking them for walkies. Eighty one per cent of canine Britons, are obese. Worse yet, Christmas is coming, the dog is getting fat, and over Christmas it will be bound to get fatter still, since you love it so much that you cannot wait to stuff it with mince pies and cake and shortbread and pudding. If its party trick is to walk on its hind legs, your guests will think its party trick is to do impressions of Nicholas Soames.

This survey has worried me, as surveys invariably do. That is what surveys are for. I am now worried about all pets at Christmas, and since the CSP has had nothing to say about how too much misguided love might affect any of the others, I feel I ought to be the one to step in here. I know, for example, what a dreadful mistake it would be to overfeed a stick insect: it survives by looking like a stick, but fatten it to a meaty twig, or possibly a lollipop, and its hours would be instantly numbered. Shake it out of its jar to, say, help you with your charade of *The Thin Red Line*, and the budgie would be on it in a trice.

Not, of course, that the budgie should be in the room in the first place. Crackers might be pulled, and since everyone always shouts out their riddle several times over, you could well be stuck with a clever boy repeatedly shrieking: 'How can you tell an elephant has been in the fridge?' so far into 2007 that, in order to preserve your sanity, you will have to kill it.

It would also be a grave mistake not to put the goldfish bowl in the loft. Christmas is a time of peculiar drinks – advokaat, kummel, chartreuse, mulled lambrusco – which may not be to everyone's, indeed anyone's, taste, and guests too polite to spit into the fire might easily seek the nearest covert receptacle. There is, I promise, little that breaks up a jolly Christmas party more effectively than a child demanding to know why Goldy has turned greeny and sunk motionless into his little coral castle.

Many of you, or at any rate your children, will have beloved gerbils and/or hamsters. So beloved, indeed, that they are encouraged to sit on shoulders, peek out of pockets, or ride hilariously around in the caboose of the Hornby Dublo train that a delighted kiddie unwrapped at dawn and set up on the living-room floor. The thing about these lovable little rodents, however, is not only that they do not always stay where they are put, but also that they are by nature highly inquisitive: they will scuttle into any appealing hole, especially if it is unfamiliar. There is, I promise, little that breaks up a jolly Christmas lunch more effectively than an elderly aunt demanding to know why her portion of stuffing appears to have four crispy legs.

Tortoises, fortunately, are easier to keep a welfare eye on, though a weather eye must be kept open now that, thanks to global warming, the weather concerned may beguile our testudinal chums into suppressing the urge to hibernate. Though not always successfully: a pet tortoise lively enough to amble about on the carpet while balloons are being exploded or 'The Green Eye of the Little Yellow God' lustily recited may, should silence fall as drunks drop off, pull in its bits and bobs and itself drift into motionless kip. The risk here, of course, is that one of the drunks might suddenly wake up and fancy a meat pie. There is, I promise, little that breaks up a comfy Christmas snooze more effectively than a beloved brother-in-law looking at five thousand quids worth of bridgework all over the rug. Pet lovers will argue that I am citing a case here where no Christmas harm has come to the cherished animal, but which of us can be certain that, on feeling its shell suddenly grabbed, the tortoise would not tragically stick its head out to see what was happening?

Hang on, I hear 23 per cent of my readership fretfully cry, what about our beloved moggies? Oh, do leave off: you of all pet lovers know that cats are canny, circumspect self-preservationists, tuned to spot trouble a mile off and keep well away. Unless, of course, they happen to live with an animal dumb enough to put a big wobbly tree up and hang bright dangly balls all over it.

Growing Pains

THIS was my plan for Tuesday morning: I was going to jump out of bed, run down to the Shaw Theatre on Euston Road, burst into the annual National Childminding Association conference, shout something from the floor, and, once I had got a reaction from the podium, run home again and write this.

Well, not this. This is what I shall have to write instead, because the plan didn't work. The Shaw Theatre was shut. The conference was over. It had lasted only a day. I don't know why the NCMA Conference is so brief, it may be because, if all the childminders are at it, there isn't anybody at home to look after their kids, but whatever the reason, all I have done this morning is jump out of bed, run down to Euston Road, bang on a big door, and run home again. I have not been able to take advantage of the delightful coincidence of their holding it at the Shaw Theatre; because what I had been planning to shout was: 'Parentage is a very important profession, but no test of fitness for it is ever imposed in the interest of children.' I wanted to shout this not just because Shaw said it when he was 90, after he had had a fair amount of time to think about it, but also because, at the distant beginning of that time, he had had a really rotten childhood, thanks to the fact that his mother was a singer with the range of a frog who selfishly pursued her unnecessary career rather than bring little George Bernard up; which – and this is the point – explains neither why he became an estate agent at 14, nor a great writer afterwards.

I would have shouted it in order to see what Dr Penelope Leach, president of the NCMA, made of it. She is a woman whose dedicated work I have not only long admired, but often relied upon: Mrs Coren and I bought her seminal *Your Baby and Child* when it came out in 1977, and frequently threw it at our two when they wouldn't shut up. Now she has come up with yet another set of mouldbreaking assertions; but, despite my continuing respect, at the core of her meticulously researched and convincingly argued case there is a major flaw which I would have taken a shy at this morning, if she and her acolytes hadn't all gone home.

The flaw was succinctly adumbrated by the headline in Monday's *Daily Mail* encapsulating as only the *Daily Mail* can Dr Leach's pre-released text for the conference: 'Children Do Best If Mother Is There.' *Mail* readers would have relished that: deployed around Warminster-on-Sea, straining through their binoculars for the first ripples of anything attempting to wade ashore to claim council houses and new hips, they must, the moment the paper was delivered to their hides, have buckled the welkin with their cheers.

Not me: I am not bothered by the socio-political resonances of Dr Leach's latest conclusion that maternal care is better than nannying, I am bothered only by the notion of better. What is a better child? Better for what? Mrs Shaw was a lousy mother. Mrs Hitler was exemplary. Put another way, were you to wish to found a great city which would develop not only into a mighty empire but also an illustrious culture blessed with immortal literature, an exemplary legal system, extraordinary art and architecture, and 307 different sorts of pasta, your best bet would be to be brought up by a wolf.

I cannot, of course, speak for myself, except to say that during my formative years I was never allowed to, my mother being a lovably strict woman for whose husband World War Two came not a moment too soon (though family rumours that he was the only member of the RAF to attempt to tunnel into Colditz are fairly wide of the mark). She did, mind, exercise her will when my own wife was pregnant: our cat used to sit on my Mrs Coren's lap, treadling her maternity smock, until my father's Mrs Coren hit it with a dish-cloth on the grounds that if it did not get off, our child would be born with feline lineaments. That he was not is a source of some gratitude to him, since a food critic walking into a flash restaurant with a ginger tail hanging out of his trousers would be less than welcome, especially if he asked for *mouse au vin*.

Oh, you know what I'm saying, Dr Leach: though you have spent your life researching comparative routes to the optimum nurturing of happiness, you and I both know that the truly scientific conclusion is that it's six of one and half a dozen of the other. And anyway, as Shaw further remarked, in *Man and Superman*: 'A lifetime of happiness! No man alive could bear it.'

Olympic Standards

'YOU'RE up early,' I said.

'When you are on a secret training run,' he said, 'you do not want people about. I have been attempting to smash the Heathrow/Hyde Park record.'

'How did it go?' I enquired.

'I got it up to 3 hours 27 minutes,' said the cabbie, through the slot. 'In sporting jargon, £171.40. But these are early days; I could well knock on ten more by going through Hounslow twice and sticking to alleys. I see the main threat as coming from the Germans, they are competitive sods, I've had 'em sat there with a map and compass before now. Where to, guv?'

'Wapping,' I said.

'There's roadworks at King's Cross,' he said. 'I'll have to go via Norwich.'

'Drop me off at the nearest Tube,' I said.

'No doubt,' said the Editor, 'you are expecting the team to concentrate on our usual two main events, the three-day SEX SCANDAL ROCKS OLYMPIC VILLAGE and the five-day DRUGS SCANDAL ROCKS OLYMPIC VILLAGE?'

'More yet, sir,' I said. 'I should also like to put myself down for the synchronised BRIBES SCANDAL ROCKS OLYMPIC VILLAGE. I feel ready.'

The Editor offered me his warmest smile. Frost formed on my stubble.

'The game has changed, old timer,' he said. 'For the 2012 Olympics, all our efforts will be bent towards achieving supremacy in one event only: the MILLIONAIRE DISCUS. This great newspaper is going to make someone the first discus millionaire. Every day, a little cardboard disc will be tucked inside the Business Section. Each – here is the brilliant part – will have a different number on it.'

'Fabulous,' I murmured. 'What can I do?'

'You can go and find a young British hopeful to interview,' he said.

'This news has come as a wonderful boost for Sharon!' barked her mother into my tape recorder. 'Only 12, but already showing every sign of the form that will take her right to the top, thanks to one of that unsung band of British mums dedicated to seeing that Rumania does not have things all its own way in 2012! Yes, the lights snap on every day at 4 a.m. behind the neat curtains of the spotless Chigwell semi with its own off-street parking and wealth of shrubs, as Doreen, 38 but with the figure of a woman half her age, ensures that Sharon goes through those rigorous exercises which will develop her lithe young body into a finely-tuned instrument in time for that fateful day seven years from now when it will be Olympic Week In the *Sun*. Sharon will be competing with the world's top stunnas for the coveted Page Three spot, leading to fab modelling contracts, and her own chat show.'

'Plus a champagne-style penthouse for the best Mum in the world,' said Sharon, to the carpet.

There was a pub opposite. I ordered a pint.

'You want to get sunnink hot inside you,' said the landlord, 'day like this. Do you a nice Athlete's Lunch: jumbo piece of Olympic Cheddar, two onions as supplied to the British relay team, slice of the only wholemeal wossname Kelly Holmes would touch, and a dollop of fencer's mustard, twelve quid.'

'Seems a bit steep.'

'It'll be fifteen tomorrow. You would not credit the anticipated demand. We are less than 12 miles from Wembley Stadium. I am going for gold.'

'But the Games are five years off,' I said.

'I might be dead in five years,' said the landlord.

'This could be his last Olympic chance,' cried a potman from the cellar.

Outside the pub, I found my way barred by a policemen's arm. A mob was running by, sweating and spitting.

'What is it?' I asked. 'A charity jog? A terror attack? An Ikea sale?'

'Who knows?' he said. 'Could be hotdog sellers, travel agents, guides, ticket touts, publishers, pickpockets, you name it. They could be rushing to audition for Celebrity Love Pole Vault, Strictly Come Shotputting, narmean?'

'Dear God!' I cried. 'Is this going to go on for another five years?'

'There's a sporting chance,' he said.

A Star Is Born

YOU cannot see me this morning, but I am hugging myself. That is because, on another morning in the not too distant future, you may very well be able to see me hugging myself. My television career is about to take off. Quite literally, thanks to Merseyside Police.

For this is the morning on which they launch their CCTV drone. I do not know how it came to be called a drone, but your Johnny Etymology is a funny cove, so leave us not waste time wondering how a bee with its feet up suddenly transmogrifies into the busiest bee of all, and instead rejoice that the skies above us will soon be buzzing with hundreds of titchy airborne cameras, scoping our every move. Because you may be sure that, when it comes to surveillance, it will be today Merseyside, tomorrow the world.

So I hug myself because, hitherto, my CCTV career has been embarrassingly sluggish. It has had its moments, but they were rare: true, I am something of a star in my local Waitrose, where security staff say it is always a joy watching me grin up at them as I reach for catsmeat or wonder animatedly whether I will get my trolley through a particularly tricky gap in Special Offer pyramids, scratching my head, rolling my eyes, giving it large, they say I am one of a kind; and the man in my off-licence, I know, never tires of me juggling lagers, even funnier, he says, now he's had colour put in, most customers just stand quietly in the queue, Mr Coren, you are a real tonic.

But, even when you take into account my handful of impromptu comedy classics – *Overfilling Tank And Petrol Running All Down Trousers*, say, or *Forgetting Pin Number At*

Lloyds Cashpoint And Man Behind Shouting, or even my more rehearsed performances, such as *Pulling Margaret Beckett Face In Betting Shop* – these are all minor gems, and have never drawn audiences larger than three. Four, if you count the myopic punter staring at the wrong screen for the 3.15 from Sandown Park.

I have never, you see, been lucky enough to be in a corner grocery when shotguns were deployed in time for nationwide exposure on *News at Ten,* I have never been visibly passed on Euston Station by a mobiling hoodie subsequently arrested for phoning Bin Laden, I have never been anywhere near when a congestion-charge camera spotted, say, Pete Doherty rooting about in a litter-bin, or an Ivy washroom lens caught Joan Collins tackling a zit. I wasn't around. In CCTV business, timing is everything.

Or, rather, has been up until now. From today, thanks to the Old Mersey Bill, and from tomorrow, thanks to the world we now live in, CCTV will be everywhere. All I have to do to go big-time is get out and about a lot. Eventually, something major is bound to happen where I am, and when it does, you will see me that very night, just behind Natasha Kaplinsky's ear. I shall be the one doing handstands.

Just A Tick

As I write, I have absolutely no idea what time it is. This is something of an inconvenience when you are working against a deadline. Suddenly, the deadline is working against you. You will say, how strange, he is a man of the world, he has knocked about a bit, why hasn't he got a watch? I will answer, good question, there are no flies on you, but the truth is I do have a watch. It is on the other side of the room, under a cushion on the chesterfield I use to stare at the ceiling when I am unable to think of anything with which to meet my deadline. It is not only under a cushion, it is also under the sweater I have put over the cushion. The only way I can find out the time is to get up from the screen at which I am tapping this, cross the room, take the sweater off the cushion and the cushion off the watch, look at it, and then put it back under all the stuff I took off it to check what time it was. This takes a lot of time you cannot spare when you have a deadline.

Especially because, willy-nilly, a neurotic factor has now introduced itself into the equation: I have become unable to not think about the time, and am thus in a constant battle with the temptation to get up and run across the room to do the thing with the watch and the cushion and the sweater. Each time I do this, of course, the time employed in doing it chips off a bit more of the time between me and the deadline. I rather think it was Richard II who put his finger bang on my button when he muttered: 'I wasted time, and now doth time waste me,' but I cannot check up on his exact words because that would mean getting up and running over to the bookshelf, and if I did that I should be incapable, as I passed the chesterfield on the way back, of not lifting up the sweater and the cushion and looking at the watch again.

You, who if I do not stop all this will soon be as nuts as I am, are entitled to an answer to your second question, which is 'Why is his watch not on his wrist?' Join me at Nice airport, yesterday at 6.11 p.m. GMT, a trip you may easily make, whatever Einstein said – you wouldn't believe how little he thought about time, compared with me – and you will see me pulling the bezel out of the side of my watch, because the hands stand at 7.11 French time, and I am soon to board a plane back to England, and I not only like to be ready – I have this thing about time, you know – I also like to have something to do at airports when I am waiting to get on a plane which is an hour late and I have finished my book. So I pulled out the bezel to turn back the hands, but what happened was, the bezel kept on coming until it was totally out. 'My bezel has come out,' I told Mrs Coren, in some distress, but she had not finished her book, so could not have been expected to look up and be the helpmeet for me, despite what God promised.

So I got up and walked across the departure lounge to a shop called Ferret, which sells duty-free watches, and I put my watch on the counter, and the Ferretwoman did one of those eye-rolling-mouth-pursing-tongue-clicking shrugs which the French learn in the womb and said that my watch was up the Swanee, albeit in French. Then, for hers is a race ever on the *qui vive* to help the afflicted, she offered to sell me a Rolex, an Omega, a Longines, or other fine item much sought after by people wishing to have their forearms chopped off while waiting to cross a Harlesden zebra, but eventually settled (slightly grudgingly, I sensed) for the cheapest of her stock, a black plastic Swatch hardly larger than a dinner-plate; so I gave her 40 euros, and hurried back to show it to Mrs Coren, who I'm sure might have brought herself to look up from her Trollope, had my happy cries been audible above the din. For Nice, as I would learn to my cost, is a very noisy airport indeed.

That cost presented itself, an hour later, at 30,000 feet, the height at which the plane, having depowered to cruising mode, went quiet. And Mrs Coren went pale. 'Something's ticking,' she said. I cocked an ear. She wasn't wrong. Somehow, something with an almighty rhythmic clunk had succeeded in getting itself aboard the plane, with the object of blowing us out of it. It was only as I reached up with my trembling left hand to press the steward's button that I clocked what it was. I had bought a watch which mice would want to run up; if it had a chime (I had owned it for only half-an-hour, and didn't know what else might sit in the huge Swatch works beneath the plate), 80 passengers would turn round, expecting *News At Ten*.

I didn't get much sleep last night. Though I put the watch on a far table, not only did its tick rattle the windows, but its luminous hands so set the wallpaper aglow as to leave me lying there thinking that if Saddam were to start building watches like this, Clare Short would volunteer for Tornado duty. Do you blame me for keeping it under a cushion under a sweater?

Gift Horses

OH, come on, for pity's sake: pity the Prince of Wales, it is the least you can do: not only do you know that the public enquiry into the whereabouts of all the gifts presented to him over the years could not have come at a worse time, you know he knows it, too, because he has a snazzy monogrammed Rolex with the date on it. Indeed, he has a dozen of them, somewhere, each snazzier than the last – though not, perhaps, as snazzy as the two hundred he used to have, before they all went walkabout – so it can hardly have escaped him that there remain very few shopping days to Christmas. We should therefore not be at all surprised if, even as he crawls around on all fours this morning, he finds himelf muttering, like an earlier melancholy prince, 'The time is out of joint; O cursed spite, that ever I was born to set it right!'

The all fours, of course, are not strictly speaking his. He does not crawl around on his own all fours, any more than he squirts his own toothpaste onto his own toothbrush or holds his own jam-jar for his own widdle; he has people who crawl around for him on their all fours. There will be several of them up in the royal loft right now, crawling fit to bust, seeking the bits and bobs that, with any luck, might have fallen behind the tanks or between the joists, groping under this and that, getting filthy, getting splinters, while he stands in the middle with his enormous hand-tooled gilt-edged crested clipboard, ticking things off. The first thing he ticked off, by the way, was the clipboard. It was a present from the Akond of Swat. Fortunately, it was for his birthday, only last Thursday; that is why he has still got it.

He has not, as the harrowing cries from the four far corners of the huge loft keep informing him, got much else. He has, for example, just discovered that he has no longer got either the life-size clockwork moose presented to him by the Saskatchewan Rotary Club to celebrate his first tooth, or the solid gold cricket bat given to him by the Sultan of Brunei on the occasion of his woodwork O-level. Coming, as these two grievous buffets did, hard upon the news that his graduation ermine duvet and matching bathmat from US Ambassador Annenberg was no less missing than the 266-piece Limoges mah jong set gifted by Emperor Bokassu for Chanukkah 1983, they have not surprisingly cast the stricken heir into even glummer depths.

The fact that the Keeper of the Loose Floorboard now lopes across the loft to inform the Prince that the return on three of these items was £768.20, less 40 per cent commission to the Highgrove window-cleaner, is scant consolation; especially as, pressed sotto voce, Floorboard is compelled to inform the Prince that the fourth, unsold, item is currently in the possession of a former Miss South Uzeira, whom Prince Andrew once invited up to the loft to inspect his etchings: determined not to leave empty-handed after terminally holing her sateen basque on the outstretched finger of an alabaster cherub presented to the Duke of Edinburgh by the 2 Para sergeants' mess, she might well turn nasty, murmurs Floorboard, should Sir Michael Peat apply for a warrant to search her dressing-room at the Stoke-on-Trent Peppermint Rhino. Glancing at his clipboard, however, HRH is unable to identify the etchings in question; upon fraught enquiry, he is told that they were a complete series of Piranesi's *Vedute*, first examples off the plate and signed by the artist, and had recently raised almost £90, which Prince Andrew had said was bloody fantastic, considering they weren't even in colour.

Since, at this news, the Prince of Wales gives out a low whimper and has to be helped onto a fortuitously unsellable skunkskin ottoman (a Thanksgiving gift of the Arkansas DAR) while Kleenex Poursuivant mops his gracious brow, let us take on him a little of the pity I besought at the beginning of all this, and tiptoe from the dreadful loft to muster the remainder of it. Why, you ask, did I say that this was the worst possible time for HRH to be forced to compile a list of all the presents he was once given? Because it is also the time when the rest of us are forced to compile lists of all the presents we are about to give. And the last fear of which any of us needs to be reminded as Christmas looms is the annually recurring one that whatever we give, the recipient won't want; a fear fully justified by the latest national statistics on which I have been able to lay my hands, which show that 31 per cent of gifts end up in lofts, 22 per cent find their way into car-boot sales, 19 per cent go to charity shops to ensure that African tribesmen will all have the same stripey tie, and 16 per cent are passed on next year to daily helps, milkmen, paperboys, and Rumanian hawkers unable to fathom a country which leaves you standing on a front step with more bathfoam than you came to sell.

Consider, then, how the sensitive Sage of Highgrove must be feeling, thrust willy-nilly into his public role as lowerer of the national morale. He has binned the gift of the Magi, and a cold coming he has had of it.

Going, Going . . .

How can I bring myself to buy duct tape? How can I walk into my local hardware shop and look Albert in the eye and say I want duct tape? How do I reply when he says, no problem, Mr Coren, what kind of duct tape, bog standard, de luxe, ultra, state-of-the-art, what's it for? I shall have to reply that it's for ducts. He will say what kind of duct, and I shall begin sweating, because I do not know what a duct is. I shall not be able to tell him it's for windows, even though he knows it's for windows, and I know that he knows. I shall have to say duct tape, duct tape, what am I thinking of, what has got into me, Albert, why did I say duct tape, what I meant was a hammer, have you got a nice one? I shall then buy a hammer, and go home again. Provided my home is still where I left it.

Bottled water? How can I bring myself to buy three months' supply of bottled water? That is 1000 bottles, even if you wash sparingly. The Waitrose girl will say are you sure, Mr Coren, it's usually two, and I will have to say we are throwing this big party for teetotallers, we have 300 of them coming over next Sunday, they can't half shift it, but she will know, and I will know that she knows, especially after I ask her for 1000 candles because I want the garden to look magic, teetotallers don't have much in their lives, candlelit Evian is as good as it gets. Oh, and it's a baked bean and sardine party, by the way, so can I have five crates of each?

Have you, too, read *Preparing For The Unexpected*? It is an Australian emergency manual, but the British Cabinet Office has suggested we download it from the the UK

Resilience website, because their own pamphlet isn't ready yet, and the days grow short as you reach whenever it is. Yes, you are dead right, pardon the expression, it is a flummoxing title, since if something is unexpected, you cannot by definition prepare for it, and what is unexpected to an Australian, anyway? A slow left-arm terrorist with an unspottable googly pitching anthrax grenades outside off-stump? A suicide kangaroo with a gas-filled pouch? A nuclear dunny? I spotted none of these, I discovered merely that what is unexpected in Oz, no doubt because it is an upside-down spot, is what is all too expected everywhere else, and you prepare for it with, ho-hum, duct tape, plastic sheeting, candles, mineral water, tinned tucker, and a portable stove or barbecue – all pretty useless, of course, unless you happen to own a supermarket. But the truly unsettling thing is that they become even more useless the further on you read.

For example, you are advised not only to hermetically seal your premises in the event of anything (un)expected happening, you are also advised to be prepared to evacuate those premises immediately it happens. Now, though I am not perhaps a household word where civil defence experts foregather, I nevertheless feel entitled to be a mite confused by this: just suppose I do become scared enough to handle the embarrassment of showing how scared I have become, how will I know when to tear off all the duct tape and sheeting which have made my newly sealed premises unevacuatable? Oh look, at the end of my street furthest from the (un)expected, neighbours are frantically sealing themselves in, but at the end nearest to it, neighbours are frantically tearing down everything they have just finished sealing themselves in with. Any second now, they will be running out carrying crates of tinnies and cartons of candles, pushing handcarts full of water, portable barbecues on their shoulders, and trailing duct tape behind them like Andrex labradors, but where will they be running?

Towards the (un)expected is where. I bet you didn't expect that, but it's what the Australians advise: 'In the event of an incident, move to an upwind location to avoid contamination.' Oh, really? If you are downwind of something nasty, surely the only way to get upwind of it is to run towards it and come out the other side? That is how wind works. If, that is, you can tell if it's working at all: I have never been any good at assessing wind-direction, I cannot count the number of occasions upon which I have licked a forefinger and stuck it up in the air to discover only that I had absolutely no idea which side of it was being blown on.

Let us instead look on a brighter side. Might there not be a touch of good old-fashioned Australian attitude behind this patently daft suggestion? Might it not really be about the best place to light a barbecue when the wind is up, and to hell with the risk of contamination? I offer this not merely as the only sensible explanation, but also because it gives me no small pleasure, amid all the current hysteria, to wonder whether the truth is that the Australians really don't give a stuff.

Christmas List

THE Rev. Lee Rayfield having told his Maidenhead flock that Father Christmas could not exist because his reindeer would have to gallop at the speed of light to get two billion sacks emptied in the time allotted, and the Bishop of Lichfield having described Jesus as an asylum-seeker and the Three Wise Men as hitmen sent by Herod to knock him off, you may be wondering what else you need to tell your children this Christmas, should they enquire. Here, then, is a short list.

WHAT ARE GLASS BALLS ALL ABOUT?

A long time ago, questioned by nasty Bethlehem media over the paternity of her little baby, a young woman admitted the possibility that the father might not have been Almighty God, she could have been the victim of a conman she might or might not have met once or twice, she couldn't be expected to remember all the details, it wasn't easy pursuing a career as a pioneer Christian aid worker while at the same time being the wife of a prominent cabinet-maker who expected a hot meal on the table every night; she was juggling a lot of balls and it was inevitable that, occasionally, one of them fell to the ground.

In this year's performances of Peter Pan, children will be told that every time a glass ball falls off the tree and shatters, somewhere a lady finds herself up the duff.

WHAT DO SPROUTS COMMEMORATE?

In biblical times, whenever there was a shortage of stones as the result of an unusually large number of women being taken in adultery and unable to think up a plausible defence, the magistrates permitted the use of raw sprouts. Indeed, since the Aramaic words for the two missiles are very similar, several commentators believe that what Jesus actually said was: 'Let him who is without sin cast the first sprout.'

WHY TURKEYS?

Turkeys were first discovered by the Pilgrim Fathers, who, noticing they wore feathers, believed them to be native Americans and therefore heathens, and understandably burnt them at the stake. Food, however, was terribly short that first winter, and since the grilling turkeys smelt jolly appetising, the pilgrims asked God for guidance and were given the all-clear, although stuffing was not mentioned. The Rev. Hector Flynn noted in his diary for December 25, 1621: 'The heathen was really moist.' The December 31 entry reads: 'Heathen risotto again.'

WHY ROBINS?

Robins are put on Christmas cards to remind us how lucky we are not to be Italian. Italian children have to eat robins at Christmas, also starlings, wrens, gulls, sparrows, budgies, owls, finches, blackbirds, and, if daddy is a bit shortsighted, hot-air balloons and microlite aircraft. If they do not eat these all up, they do not get a tangerine in their stocking, they get a horse's head.

WHY DID THE ANGEL OF THE LORD COME DOWN?

We cannot be certain, but the likeliest explanation is that an Italian was on a Bethlehem winter break.

WHY DID THREE SHIPS COME SAILING BY?

Seeing three ships come sailing by on Christmas Day in the

morning is a sign of good luck. It means that the one carrying 30 million poundsworth of nice new luxury motor cars has not collided with a second one and then been run into by a third.

WHO FIRST DREAMT OF A WHITE CHRISTMAS?

Irving Berlin. When the Berlin family arrived in New York from Russia, they were so poor they had to live in Harlem, where Irving was four feet too short to play basketball. One Christmas Eve, the lonely teenager was staring miserably out of the window watching the neighbourhood kids slam-dunking, when his father asked him what he was dreaming of. Pretty soon, the family was so rich it could move to a lovely big house on Long Island, where Irving took up golf.

IS THERE ANYTHING WE SHOULD KNOW ABOUT THE CHRISTMAS PUDDING?

Yes. The Bishop of Lichfield has already explained about Herod's funny little homicidal ways, but you may not know that it was something that ran in the family. Bringing in the Christmas pudding commemorates his daughter Salome's serving him John the Baptist's head on a plate. The rumour that her father was not as pleased as he might have been because he couldn't find the threepenny-bit should be ignored: the traditional insertion of a coin dates from Christmas 1649, when, to express everybody's gratitude for the decapitation of King Charles I, Cromwell's Auntie Doreen, in a gesture of unprecedented Puritan frivolity, poked a groat into his yuletide bap.

Lie Back And Think of Cricklewood

COULD I have got into bed with H. G. Wells? Those little bandy legs. That pot belly. A moustache flecked with his favourite nibble, jellied eels. It would be like kissing an otter.

Or Bertrand Russell? All very nice, strolling into the Café Royal on the arm of a celebrity liable to come out with 'Matter is a convenient formula for describing what happens where it isn't' and get all the sommeliers stamping and whistling, but at some point in the evening you would be bound to find that long beak in your ear and a skinny hand whipping up your thigh like a concupiscent crab.

Or Napoleon? Haemorrhoids, as I recall. Or would, no question, were I about to squirt a couple of rounds of Numero Cinq onto my heaving balcon and turn back the eiderdown. And there was also the unusually small matter of that desiccated relict in its tiny casket which came under the Sotheby's hammer a few years back. Not much tonight, Josephine, one gathered.

Now, were you – a long shot – Professor Irving Davies of the University of Wisconsin, you would find it odd that, in a long fantasy life, none of the above had ever occurred to me. As most men, I imagine, I have seen myself as most men I imagine: I have been up Everest, round the Horn, over the top, behind the stumps, before the mast, between the posts, under the volcano, and am possibly the only man ever to have dreamed of being the author of Walter Mitty. But I have never yet wondered what it would be like to be a mistress, and it is this that Professor Davies would find odd, since he has just presented a paper to a major shrink conference, identifying 'the common male fantasy of reincarnating as a kept woman'.

Lawks-a-mercy, Professor, you do know how to turn a girl's head! Having never thought about this before, I now find it hard to think about anything else. What sort of woman would I come back as, petite or voluptuous? There is much to be said for being miniature and thus likelier to kindle the protective flame, but if I were petite I should have to be pert, and I cannot see myself as pert. If I were voluptuous I should have only to be dumb, and it is a lot easier being dumb. Then again, I might run to fat a lot more quickly than if I were petite; I should have to diet to keep the man who was keeping me, and there's no logic in reincarnating as the desideratum of someone eager to stand me 14 courses at the Gavroche if I have to stick to Ryvita and Perrier to hold him. Alternatively, I could plump for something a mite more recherché. Recherchée. History's roster of concubinage is pockmarked with the *jolie laide,* which, for the poorer linguists among you, is of course French for jolly laid. Jósephine Beauharnais had a goatee, Emma Hamilton was built like a Martello Tower, Traudl Mühler-Röstow had a squint so divergent that the Prussian junkers who flocked to her boudoir were all too frequently not the ones she had had her eye on, while the fact that George Sand could easily be mistaken for George Sanders mattered not a fig to top bananas like Alfred de Musset and Frédéric Chopin, who could have had their pick of midinettes with the sort of figures that would get Trappist monks tunnelling under the wire. Yes, all things considered, I think that's me settled.

But still unsettled, too. What of my ideal man? You will have gathered from my opening remarks that I have misgivings about being Lady Ottoline Coren, or Mrs Patrick Coren, or even The Cricklewood Lily: rubbing shoulders with the great is all very well, but it doesn't stop at shoulders, and the vast majority of the great, then and now, strike me as satyriatical ratbags of a highly unprepossessing order. I do not wish to be taken briefly and peremptorily between division bells or first and second halves / rounds / acts / races / wickets / courses / guitar solos, these representing a fair sample of the working environment for a girl like me. Nor, though I enjoy *The Desert Song* as much as the next girl, do I fancy returning as a common law Begum Aga Coren, spending all day mooching around a requisitioned floor of the Dorchester with Number 89 on my back, waiting to be tannoyed into service. And as for aiming any higher, it should, I think, be made clear that if I had to come back as Camilla Parker Coren, I wouldn't go in the first place.

What remains? Droning barristers, ponderous telly-pundits, unctuous quacks, preening chefs, honking bankers, celebrity gardeners, viagrated tycoons . . . face it, girls, when you come right down to it, what I'd really be looking for would be some hunky bald sexagenarian with GSOH and several of his own teeth who knows how to treat a lady and doesn't kiss and tell. Quite what Professor Davies would conclude from that, however, I shrink from imagining.

Shelf Life

MY new stamping ground is quite unlike my old stamping ground. In the high and far-off times, Best Beloved, when I stamped the Cricklewood ground, peeking through this nocturnal window and that, the faces were all screenlit by *EastEnders*. Here they are all screenlit by their next novel. In my old local, men wept into their Guinness and cursed their foremen; in my new one, they weep into their Chablis and curse their agents. In my old betting shop, the punters queued to back horses; in my new one, they queue to back each other: they are not interested in the Cesarewitch or the Lincoln or the Oakes, only in the Booker and the Whitbread and the Somerset Maugham. Oh, look, there is Beryl Bainbridge, about to lay a pony on A. N. Wilson, who is waiting behind her with an earful of mobile, getting the SP on Melvyn Bragg. Who is sucking his pencil at the counter, wondering if the going suits Margaret Forster, who is sitting in the window, watching the tic-tac man across the street signal the odds on Martin Amis. Who is by the wall, squinting through his rollie-smoke at Beryl Bainbridge, checking her fitness.

In short, this is a booky spot: a square half-mile packed to the chattering gunwales with people who write books, review books, broker books, tout books, publish books, sell books, and – fortunately for all of these – buy and read books. And each and every one of them, producer and consumer alike, is bibliomaniacally competitive. They are all fixated on the dread that someone might be bookier than they are. Which is why a glittering booky couple about to quit this place have, willy-nilly, bequeathed it a passing shot that is felling casualties on every side.

Mr and Mrs Michael Frayn are decamping from Primrose Hill for Richmond. Having sold up, they are packing up, but while the former has merely made their neighbours glum, the latter is driving them nuts. Because Michael, in a newspaper interview, let slip that the biggest headache of the move was encrating their 250 metres of books. And seconds after this news broke, through every local window issued a low and terrible keening, punctuated by the snap of steel-measuring tapes whizzing back, time and again, into their little cases. But not enough times or agains: for through those same windows the residents could see the Post Office tower, a mile away, and torture themselves with the thought that the Frayn library was taller: stacked, it would have clouds on it. And they have just measured their own, to discover that it would come not even half-way up.

It is the meterage that has thrown us into a tizzy. Hitherto, we have measured books in numbers, since the most important thing about literature is, of course, how many bits of it you have got: 5000 is smug, 8000 is preening, 2000 derisory, and so on. So it was extremely important to know how many books the Frayns owned to see how we ourselves shaped up against a benchmark of the paragon litterati. But meterage frustrates this utterly: people are mooching Primrose Hill, wondering, for example, if the Frayns keep only hardbacks. Were this so, they might have a scant 4000, if the books were really fat (e.g. do they keep all their old copies of *Who's Who?)*, which would be pretty unimpressive against our 7000 paperbacks, though these occupy only 97 metres. And do they keep their phone-books on the bookshelves, and if so are they flat, taking up thrice the space, and are their very tall books flat, too, atlases and art books and cookbooks and gardening manuals, and if not, are they upright and slanted, and is Frayn including the space left by the slant?

Then again, since we are talking about two major readers here, how many of their books are duplicated? Michael might well have popped into Daunts to buy something, even while Claire was forking out for the self-same book in Hatchards. What about the books neither of them paid for? Surely review copies shouldn't count, or signed copies brought round to dinner by friends too stingy to buy a bunch of flowers? Where do we stand on three metres of *Encyclopaedia Britannica* or the *OED*, are these four dozen books or merely one of each? Can I make myself believe the Frayns have the complete 572 Barbara Cartlands and cannot bring themselves to bin them rather than ship them to Richmond, never mind the quality, feel the width? But if they have brought themselves to do that, then how many more metres than 250 might they have binned or Oxfammed? There could have been unimaginable lengths of Blyton, Archer, football annuals, AA books, Gideon bibles; the unwinnowed Frayn collection might well have stood higher than the Empire State.

See, the crates are sealed, the van is chugging up Gloucester Terrace; I shall never know, now. But what the hell: it is Richmond's turn to measure and gnash.

The Folks Who Live On The Hill

If you think I do not give a fig for Jude Law, you are mistaken. We are all communities, these days, and since he is my Primrose Hill neighbour, I must be there for him. That, five years ago, I went there for me is neither here nor there; nor is the observation that you would not expect a man called Jude Law to end up on Primrose Hill: you would expect a man called Jude Law to end up on Boot Hill. A man called Jude Law should be a mythic bounty hunter with a Colt on his hip and a Derringer in his hat, riding into some rickety wooden town at high noon, bent on cashing in on the head of Jesse James, only to find that Jesse has a hip and a hat of his own, and also, as a lay preacher, knows a thing or two about the quick and the dead.

But on Primrose Hill, the real Jude Law is alive. And kicking. That is what caught the attention of the press, who gleefully reported his booting out of his fiancée Sienna, following his discovery that she was knocking off his best friend Daniel Craig. The press did it gleefully because it was only recently that they had reported Sienna's booting out of Jude for knocking off Daisy Wright. Sienna was particularly ratty because Daisy was their nanny, but let me say in my neighbour's defence that if Miss Wright comes along, a chap cannot pass up his chance of happiness on the meagre grounds of taste.

So then, is this *Jeu d'esprit* just about spooky names? Well, yes, especially if we take into account the icy fingers of Sadie Frost, formerly Mrs Law, which sent a shiver down the spine of her busily bi-lateral neighbour Kate, the neighbourhood's rolling Moss who, though she may not as yet have gathered any Stones, has certainly come tumbling down Primrose Hill and broken a fair few of the crowns that reign over her feckless community. (Amateur paparazzi wishing to make a bob or two with their snapping cellphones will find them holding court outside, where else, The Queens.)

And in all this there is a yet spookier name to address. It is Primrose Hill itself. Which, when I got here, was a rather different community, one that is now, as you might guess, not entirely happy with recent changes: it had grown accustomed to preening itself for being an idyllic literary backwater – part deep, part shallow – where a blissful riparian peace, all too rare in London, was disturbed only by the plangent ping from a platen as Alan Bennett or Michael Frayn or Claire Tomalin or Martin Amis or Beryl Bainbridge or A. N. Wilson or Simon Jenkins reached the end of yet another immemorial line. The community even tolerated the odd arriviste wag, on the pitiably optimistic grounds that he might one day come to his senses and try his hand at a novel.

What, however, took us all horribly by surprise, a short while back, was the sudden headlong anabasis from West London of film folk: not only actors and directors and producers gobbling up big houses, but, gobbling up titchy flats, best boys and gaffers and grips. Primrose was the new Notting. Bang went the hood: not because these people were in pictures – many members of the community, after all, live in hope that one day their dog-eared treatment of *Northanger Abbey* will be made into a film – but because they were flash, raucous, promiscuous, assortedly bent, and thus comprehensively threatened the good name of Primrose Hill.

Well, I cannot deny that Primrose Hill is a good name. Certainly it is a better name than Greenbury Hill, which is what it was called in October 1678, when Sir Edmund Godfrey JP was found on it with a sword sticking out of him and his neck broken. Though a confidant of Charles II, the hapless Godfrey had been falsely tainted with involvement in the Popish Plot – in which the King rightly did not believe, having seen through the perjury of Titus Oates (great name, should have been a model, actor, boyband), but went along with for a quiet though merry life squeezing oranges – and, as the result, was done to death on Greenbury Hill in order to keep anti-Catholic sentiment alive. His murderer was never found, but three sad civil service pawns at Somerset House were fitted up for it. Their names? Green, Bury, and Hill. Let nobody say Protestants lack a sense of humour.

It preferred to be called Primrose Hill, after that. So the neighbourhood hasn't really gone downhill at all, has it? Convoluted celebrity wickedness is in its best tradition: puffed and reckless libertines have always trod the Primrose path of dalliance. I tell you, it wasn't like this in Cricklewood.

Poles Apart

THE Home Office has published a phrasebook aimed at helping new immigrants to express themselves in 'common media English'.

Mrs L. D. Prozniwicz,
43 Glummprospekt, LODZ

Dear Mother:
We deeply regret any inconvenience caused due to not writing before, but we are up to our eyes in the wrong kind of backlog. I trust you and Father are keeping well, remember 4 out of 5 so-called tension headaches are really due to constipation. I have found a nice bleeding room in Palmers Green, know what I mean? It has got brown linoleum, which I sleep on due to not being abreast of the situation of unfolding the camp bed. No excuses, the lad just could not put it together on the night. I am sick as the moon.

As a first-time writer, Mother, but a long-time fan, could I make this point? Isn't it about time we moved the playing-fields to make level goalposts, stopped knocking the M25, and bought back the birch? On a different note, you will be glad to learn that despite renewed pressure on the major banks and slack trading in gilts, I am eating well, thanks to a unique biological action which 8 out of 10 owners prefer. There is also a funky tin bath down the corridor, but it does not have a door on the side to step through as advertised on TV, so I do not know how to use it yet. When time is right, I may have to throw caution to winds, grasp nettle, and go in at deep end.

A Lodz reader writes to ask if I have met any girls in England yet. Well, Mrs L. D. Prozniwicz, the bubbly stunna tipped by the tabloirazzi as the next Mrs Y. W. Prozniwicz stepped into the limelight for the first time yesterday! But stacked 19-year-old Chablisse, checkout diva at a major branch of the billion-pound agglomerate Tesco, refused to be drawn on future plans. Asked by Mr Y. W. Prozniwicz what she was doing on Saturday night, she struck him with a giant economy Whiskas, perfect for whites and coloureds alike.

Speaking about the incident later from his cutting-edge lino suite, the victim, who is off the critical list, comfortable, as well as can be expected, and hoping to resume his playing career as soon as doctors give the thumbs-up to one of Britain's brightest prospects for many a long year, said: 'This violence must stop, Mr Blair, it is sending young people entirely the wrong message, I am not alone in the unshakeable conviction that unless something is done, and done soon, then nothing is going to be done about it.'

Chablisse, however, was unrepentant. 'No is still the best contraceptive. At the end of the day I hope to become involved in a caring one-to-one leg-over relationship to die for, and I want the future Mr Right to respect me as a person.' We say: COME OFF IT, CHABLISSE! Think outside your box! The people of Palmers Green have been fobbed off with this kind of spin for far too long. In the final analysis, they have earned the right to a square deal.

As if confirmation were required, later that same evening a foxy young Pole, unable to locate the keys to his fashionable lower-ground penthouse, attempted to climb through a window but was felled by a state-of-the-art, if controversial, truncheon. Struck over the head twice in one day! Just coincidence? A cynic might say yes, but then how do you explain the Loch Ness Triangle, or what Wing Co. Johnny 'Johnny' Johnny, an ex-public schoolboy with three kills to his credit, heard that night over Dortmund?

PC Dixon takes a different view. 'I have got nothing against any of them personally, and it is contrary to procedure to smack little foreign buggers, but he could have had anything under that cap. And no, the solution is not to arm the police – if I had shot him you would not believe the paperwork. Nor is voluntary repatriation the answer: the inevitable result would be that honest coppers would find theirselves knocking English people about.'

Well, Mother, that about wraps it up, the old clock on the wall is telling yours truly to take account of what is staring all of us in the face, that this is the bottom line. Suffice it to say it is the result we came for, your loving son, Y. W. Prozniwicz, News At Ten, Palmers Green.

PS: If you are affected by any issues raised in this letter, such as being Polish and not able to read it, there is a helpline on 0870 888 9992.

Rhinestones Are Forever

*A*NNOUNCING *that MI5 would, for the first time, be placing recruiting ads in newspapers, a spokesman said: 'The service is open to everyone. We are not looking for anything out of the ordinary.'*

The Guardian

Bond lifted his leg fairly athletically, for him, and buffed his left toecap behind his right shin. Then, hardly wobbling at all, he did the same with his right toecap. This made his new £59.95 brown brogues by Lilley & Skinner of Brent Cross come up very nicely. He glanced down to test whether he could see his face in them, but his gold-style Boots BOGOF spectacles had misted slightly from the stairs, so he removed them and polished them on his old school tie. A wry smile played about his lips as he reflected that if the headmaster of East Willesden Comprehensive had caught him doing it, he would not, these days, have clipped his ear. Had he tried it, Bond, who had now reached page 18 of *Teach Yourself Karate,* would almost certainly have been able to give him quite a serious push.

He knocked on the mahogany door, and entered. A plump woman behind the gleaming Ikea desk was attending to a pimple. 'The name's Bond,' he said. 'Jim Bond.' There was a hatstand in one corner, and he flicked his brown John Lewis trilby towards it.

'Your hat's gone out of the window,' said the woman.

'I've got another one,' Bond quipped effortlessly, after he had recovered. 'Can I go in now?'

She folded her compact, got up, went through intercommunicating doors, came back a few minutes later, and nodded. Bond coolly shot his Marks & Spencers cuffs, but one stuck on his Timex. The other cufflink broke.

'Ah, Bnod,' said M. 'Welcome to MI5. Congratulations on being one of the 1000 short, plain, and very ordinary agents we have, as you obviously saw in our recent newspaper advertisements, decided to recruit.'

'Not Bnod, sir,' said Bond. 'Bond. B-O-N-D.'

'It says Bnod on your application,' said M, waving it.

'I've only just started computers,' explained Bond. 'Two fingers. But any day now I expect to be able to do that thing where I reprogram one three seconds before it blows the Earth up. I bought a book at Dixon's.'

'Moneypenny tells me your hat's in the street,' said M.

'It's all right,' said Bond. 'My mum sewed my name in it. Also "If found, please return to MI5 and oblige".'

M looked at him for a time. 'It's a pity you're not Bnod,' he said finally. 'We were rather hoping you were Russian. Do you speak it?'

'Not entirely,' replied Bond. 'But j'ai un GCSE in French, sir. M'sieu.'

'Let's go and see Q,' said M. 'He'll kit you out with an MI5 hat.'

'Will it have a gun in it that fires when you blow your nose?' asked Bond. 'Or is it the sort you throw at bars and electrocute Chinamen with?'

'You're not licensed to kill,' said M. 'You're licensed to jot stuff down in your MI5 exercise book. If attacked, you're licensed to shout "Help!" Do not throw things or we'll have Health & Safety all over us.'

In the basement, Q said: 'Hello, Bond, we're just fitting out your car.'

'With rocket launchers and a passenger ejector and retractable wings?'

'No, we're just pushing the seat forward. You're rather shorter than we've been used to. What sort of dangle-dolly do you use?'

'Dice would make sense,' said Bond. 'They would impress the better casinos, when I'm off to play *chemin-de-fer* with glamorous international women spies so's I can bed them for secrets about where Mr Big is etc.'

'It'll have to be bingo,' said M, 'on our budget. You might run into a cleaner who's found something in a bin. Can't pick up hotel bills, mind.'

'They could do it in the Lada,' suggested Q. 'One of the seats goes fairly flat. By the way, here's your special MI5 pen.'

'What does it squirt?' enquired Bond. 'CS gas? Nitric acid? Curare?'

'Ink,' said Q. 'We can't crack it. Wear a blue shirt, is my advice. And this is your special MI5 disposable cigarette lighter.'

'Containing a tiny satellite phone?'

'Containing fluid for 200 lights, in case you're stuck in the dark. When it runs out, don't just chuck it away, bring it back here and sign a chitty.'

'And don't use it for cigarettes,' put in M, sternly. 'Remember, smoking can harm you and those around you.'

'I was rather hoping for a gold Dunhill fag-case, sir,' said Bond, 'that I could slip into a pocket next to my heart to deflect bullets.'

M pressed the lift-button.

'In your dreams,' he said.

Hair Today

YOU will all, I know, recall the ear with four legs. How could you not? It scuttled through your worst nightmares. In many of them, indeed, it will not only have scuttled through, it will have run up the clock; and when the clock struck one, you will have jack-knifed upright, clutching your sweat-stained duvet, for it had also struck terror into your waking heart.

That is because, though the ear was human, its four legs actually belonged to the mouse beneath it: it was both an ear with four legs, and a mouse with an ear, neither of which made for easeful sleep. It was one of the most telling images of the twentieth century, and what it was telling us was to watch out for the twenty-first one, because the four-legged ear was only the start and what the finish might be, none dared speculate. In truth, so compelling was the image that it has driven all memory of the story itself out of my head: I know it was about genetic modification, but I cannot now remember whether the object had been to create a mouse with really terrific hearing, the ear being ten times bigger than the mouse's own titchy two, or to grow ears for people whose own had fallen off. Either way, it did not make it any less daring to speculate: genes being the retentive little johnnies they are, the successful experiment might lead (a) to a race of rodents able to hear cats and ratcatchers coming ten miles away, which could usher in a global Hamelin impervious to piping, because there would never be enough tin whistles to go round, or (b) to a race of newly eared human beings genetically endowed with the capacity to breed ten times a year, who would not merely, within a few gobbling months, overrun the planet and eat everything on it, but also make a hell of a nocturnal racket, thanks to being big and strong enough, as they frantically foraged, to send dustbin lids flying.

And what I ask today is: where is that ear now? Is it still around? Are there others? What have its manufacturers been up to since? Geneticists do not stand still: might there be quadruped noses out there somewhere, or human livers waiting to be transplanted just as soon as the scientists have cracked what to do about the tail? We do not know, and I think we should be told: certainly I should, because something else murine has just happened which touches me closely, and it is extremely important for me to find out as soon as possible whether it is a good something or a bad something.

Now, when it comes to the currently must-have genetic debate, the one about modified crops, I feel, selfishly perhaps, that I can stand safely on the sidelines and choose not to be touched by it – always provided a strong wind isn't blowing, and the daffodils I can see this morning from my attic window do not come up, next spring, as broccoli. I can, in short, choose not to eat, drink, sniff or wear anything that has been fiddled with, since there will, with any luck, always be alternatives which haven't. However, Dr George Cotsarelis of the University of Pennsylvania Medical Center in Philadelphia – motivated, perhaps, not by GM ambition alone but also by the resonant incumbency of being a Greek who earns his crust in the city of brotherly love – has today announced a therapeutic breakthrough which will make millions of his fellow-men throw their hats in the air in joyous gratitude. Revealing, as they do so, exactly why they are throwing them.

For the millions are bald, and what George has discovered is how to isolate the stem cells in the follicles of genetically modified mice that can regenerate after being planted in the scalp. Crucially, the cells were from adult mice, which normally cannot form new hair follicles, and the same holds true for humans: no new hair follicles form after we are born. Though I once had a barnet that could buckle steel combs, after the follicles packed their little bags I needed only a feather duster for perfect grooming. Which, until George broke his astounding news in yesterday's papers, I had ruefully accepted as a given. Or, rather, as a taken.

So what do I do now? Dr Cotsaleris admits that this treatment will not be available to human beings for five years, but since by that time my sideburns may well have fallen out too, today is not too soon to be thinking about my stance. Shall I now cleave GM to my bosom in unqualified acceptance of the wonderful boon it is? Or must I sideline all selfish considerations and hold fast to my altruistic concerns about Pandora's box?

Later, maybe. First I have to forget that four-legged ear: come 2009, it's only hair I want to see sprouting from the top of of my head.

Einstein Gets The Bird

A MAN goes into a doctor's surgery. His face is painted bright blue, he has a banana in one ear and a gherkin in the other, a pink chrysanthemum sticking out of each nostril, and a parrot on his head. The doctor says: 'Good morning, what appears to be the trouble?' and the parrot replies: 'How do I get this thing off my feet?'

Yes, you are not wrong, it is an old joke. The important question is: how old? If any senior reader heard it more than 50 years ago, it would make me immensely grateful if he or she would write to tell me so, because should the joke have been in existence on March 14, 1954, it is quite possible that Albert Einstein, whose 75th birthday that was, told it to his birthday present. He would have done this in order to cheer his birthday present up. We do not know why his birthday present was unhappy – among other things, it is quite possible that it had not wanted to be given to Albert Einstein, and many of us might sympathise with that – we know only that Einstein's last girlfriend, Johanna Fantova, recorded the fact in her diary, which recently came to light when somebody opened a Princeton cupboard. Jotted in spidery longhand German, the text revealed that Einstein's 75th birthday present was a parrot, which he christened Bibo. He then observed it for a time, and came to the conclusion that the bird was depressed.

Now, some of you who have knocked about a bit might be tempted to the conclusion that what depressed the birthday present was not just that it had been given to Albert Einstein, but that Albert Einstein had called it Bibo, because you know that a parrot has no lips, and thus cannot do plosives. Bibo could not pronounce his new name. Albert would come in of a morning, whip back the cover, tap the cage, and say: 'Hello, Bibo, who's a pretty boy, then?', hoping that Bibo would reply 'Bibo.' Bibo could not; had he tried, anything struggling through his beak would have come out 'Gigo'. Guessing that if that happened, the smartest man in the world might conclude that he had been given the dumbest parrot in the world, Bibo said nothing. He just looked glum. I think we can all understand that.

Einstein, however, apparently couldn't. He may have been the smartest man in the world when it came to relativity, clock paradox, black holes, quantum mechanics, operationalism, or anything else on the long list I have just looked up in *The Big Boy's Book of Science Stuff*, but when it came to parrots, he was thicker than two short Plancks – a joke which seemed to me to be lying around there somewhere, even though I have not the faintest idea what it might mean. And that is the point: what Einstein did to cheer up the parrot to whom he'd given a name he didn't have the nous to realise the parrot couldn't say, was to tell it jokes the parrot couldn't comprehend.

Because what Einstein demonstrably failed to grasp was that the whole parrot/human thing works only when the parrot says words it doesn't understand but that the human being laughs at: a depressed human being may well be cheered up if a parrot shouts: 'Half a gound of tuggeny rice!' over and over again, but a depressed parrot will not be cheered up if a human being tells it the one about a man with a blue face going into a doctor's surgery.

I really don't know what Einstein thought he was playing at. Now, while I should be the first to admit that it is also undeniable that I really don't know what he thought he was playing at when he was playing at the unified field theory and all that other stuff, in the matter of the relativity between men and parrots, I feel fully qualified to have a go at him. More yet, I feel a columnar incumbency to have that go: for we live, as I think you may have spotted, in somewhat precarious times, not only because Albert's conclusion that $E=mc^2$ will any day now empower some sick dupe with a bulging tote-bag to flatten Manchester, but also because of the exponential burgeoning of scientists excitedly hurling their brains at everything from breeding fatherless mice and insisting that they stick to a low-cholesterol diet and lay off Old Navy Shag, to shredding the ozone layer with spaceships designed to land on Betelgeuse in an attempt to contact beings who may have invented a better moustrap; but while they are all, I'm sure, not only extremely bright but also wonderful to their mothers, they may well be unnervingly short of the common sense that persuades the rest of us to think twice before telling jokes to parrots.

Child's Play

IT'S no fun being a kid, these days. I know this because, as a million kids this morning hand in homework essays on what they did on Bank Holiday, one is explaining that his blew out of the window. I found it.

Today I went for a ride on my new bycicle. My dad bort it becaus my boddy-mass index was .002 per cent too high on Friday, and my Mum started screeming yu hav eeten a toffy, nigel, who gave yu the toffy, i cannot let yu out of my site for a second, what did he look like, did he tuch yu, if so wear? Nobody gave me a toffy i replide, my increesed wate is probly on acount of particulates falling out of the sky onto me wile i was in the gardn, or a grothe inside me due to passiv smoaking from Mr Foskett acros the rode, last thersday my windo was open and so was his, or maybe some hewy fleas jumped on me off of a nurban fox. At this, my dad stagger and grab the fridge for suport, seting off the alarm (yu are not alowed to tuch the fridge between meels), i hav told yu not to go into the gardn unacompnied, he cri, ilegal imgrants mite hav cut the razer-wire in the nite, yu culd end up in tieland as a yunuk slave or in a nafgan traning camp or in irak with boms tied round yu.

It is a nise bycicle. It is bolted to the flore in our sellar and there is a screen in front of it showing a video of Hamsted High Street, it is just like being their exept i wuld not have ecg wires stuk to me monitring my hart. I wear a helmet in case my seet belt snaps and i slip off, or somthing drops on me off of the seeling, my mum says yu never kno wear a spiders feet hav been, also it culd be poisonus, even waitrows cannot be sure they hav not cum into this cuntry on a norganic banana.

It is okay in the sellar, there is no windo for jerms, diesl funes, pollen, dedly wosps, chernobil stuff or terrists to get in thruogh, and there is a fone in case the blud pressure machine on my arm shows more than 100 over 60. It is not a sellphone of corse, because i am not alowed to hav brane canser, and it does not take incumming calls due to hewy breething. After i peddled 10 kilometers as recomended by the departmant of helth, i foned my mum and she unlokked the door and chekked my pulse and gave me my snak. It was a hoam-made spinich lolly with 8 calries.

i was alowed into the gardn after that, becaus it was time for my swim, i say swim, it is more of a paddel, because my dad puts only two sentimeters of water in the pool, after he has boyled the impuritys away, and even then i hav to wear a mask and snorkle, i do not mind because it wuld be hard to swim with the chane on anyway. The chane is fixed to a concreat blok, in case my father hav to run into the hous for any reason and leeve me aloan. i also hav to carry an umbrella wen i paddel, due to pidgen droppings, you can get ashthma and go blind and fail gese.

After lunch (lettice patties and non-bacterial yogurt, 31 calries) my best frend james from next dore came round. After sining my dad's clipboard and showing him the noat from there solister, his parents wated until my dad had body-searched him in their presents and put him thruogh our scanner, and then james and me went to play french crickit. It is quite a dangeruos game, one of yu has a batt made of biodegradable carboard and the other one thros a sponge at his iegs. if it hits his legs, he is out. He is then examined for dammidge by a same-sex parent in the presents of a qualfied witniss (today it was Mr Simson JP MBE from no. 64), and it is his tern to be in. This does not mean he has wun, yu are not alowed to win or loose, exitement can releese fatty asids into the sistem, you get an emblism and fail gese.

Then we climed into into my tree-hous and had tee. It is easy to clime into becaus it is on the ground, as reqired by Helth & Safety Exective Para 3317, but yu can see the tree thruogh the window, if you put on dark goggles and sunscreen factor 800. Tee was a norganic collieflour chees without chees, due to clesterol clogging your vanes, then we went inside and watched tee vee. A bit dull, due to wear it was switched off on account of posible vilence cumming on, also rays cumming out and giving yu sindromes.

Then james said culd we go to the park, and my mum fainted, and dad said it was time james went hoam, and he e-mailed his parents and they drove round from next dore in the 4wd to pik him up, so i had to play subutio on my own, but my mum sed yu cant be spers as wel as chelsey, all that flikking will give yuor forfinger reptive strane injry, yu will not be abel to text for help if a man gives yu sweets, so i went upstares and rote this hoamwork.

Victory Role

YOU cannot comprehend the awesome power which lies, this very second, in my right forefinger. Even though it is not moving: it is my left forefinger which is tapping this. Its right-hand buddy is poised, motionless save for an unavoidable tremor, over the telephone keypad beside my screen. Were it to tap just eight digits, the uncontrollable consequences could be momentous: the finger could make Mr Cresswell from Number 6 a superstar and it could make Lord Montagu jump for joy, but it could also make my parents turn in their graves. That is the power which lies in my right forefinger. It is, truly, the Fickle Finger of Fate: all it has to do is tap 8233 6539.

Even without being dialled, does that number ring a bell? It is the number for James Rowat, of ITV, who is 'seeking colour home movie footage of VE-Day to mark the 60th anniversary of the end of the war in Europe. *VE-Day in Colour* will construct a picture of May 8, 1945.' Readers, I have that footage: it is in the cupboard behind me, right now, a dozen feet away, on a tin reel, 18 minutes-worth of it, spliced together from four titchier reels by my Uncle Syd, who shot it on an 8mm Kodak in the front garden of Number 12, Oakdale; whither – were I to let my fingers do the walking – millions of gawping eyes could soon be tellyported.

Where the first thing they would see would be Mr Cresswell from Number 6 silently hopping on one leg around the rockery with a pint of Guinness on his head. The second thing they would see would be Mr Cresswell from Number 6 coming back around the rockery the other way, pintless this time and walking on his hands. For Uncle Syd was an inspired splicer: he knew how to strike a keynote. Nothing could better announce that the war was over than those two joyful journeys of Mr Cresswell from Number 6.

The scene now shifts to the porch, where a man younger than my son, in RAF blue serge, is kissing a woman younger than my daughter, in a floral frock. The small thing beside them holding a scroll is their son. After several seconds' prompting by a disembodied directorial hand, the son unrolls the scroll so that Cecil B. de Syd can wobble his camera closer and reveal that I have been given the scroll by King George VI for helping him defeat Hitler. I still have the scroll; it will come in useful if Giles ever climbs onto my knee to ask his daddy what he did in the war.

Now, ITV viewers, should the finger ever give them the chance, may feel that the sudden lurching pan from the king's scroll to the milkman's horse is a bit brusque; but the timing of United Dairies was ever a law unto itself, and there was no way an auteur as spry as Uncle Syd was going to pass up the telling chronography of the little union flag stuck to each of the horse's blinkers, nor the larger one on its backside as it trundled on from our front gate to Number 14's – and what a bonus lies fortuitously in the background of that wonky arc! A veritable bonsai Beaulieu: my father's maroon Riley Merlin, Syd's blue Wolseley Hornet, a couple of unattributable black Morris 8s, and the great green Humber Vogue outside Number 18, with Mr Paige, forever panting and forever young, buffing it to a gleam which flashes the sun back into Syd's unhooded lens, for all the world like one of the suddenly superannuated searchlights on the green at the top of our road.

Why, then, should my right forefinger still hover? Is this not only exactly the kind of stuff ITV is after, demotic history, unsung heroes, old frocks, old cars, old manners and mores, pebble-dash walls and sunburst gates and funny haircuts, a yesteryear feelgood factor resurrected to cheer these feelcrap times, but also, for me and my forefinger, a chance to stick one on Old Father Time and immortalise the dear departed?

Yes, it is; and that is the problem. For, as the film clacks on through the sprockets, so the day wanes and wearies: oh, look, here is Mr Cresswell from Number 6, face down in the rockery now, with Mrs Cresswell shouting at him, here is the milkman's horse coming back up Oakdale and doing something Uncle Syd found irresistible, here is an uncannily silent hokey-cokey showing what happens to nice suburban ladies after one bottled Bass too many, here is my father up to something extremely silly with a couple of oranges . . .

Here, in short, is unedited immortality, and it is owed a debt. I typed that sentence, you should know, with my right forefinger. It is back, like the film in the cupboard, where it belongs.

Almost a Gentleman

YOU would not, 1500 years ago today, have found me pecking spasmodically at the dawn keyboard.

You would – but only if you had been minded to abseil riskily from a rampart and squint through a loophole – have found me having a net: that is, rehearsing a few top swishes at a big wooden dragon with my burnished broadsword, the gelid flagstones of my bedchamber ringing to the twinkling sabatons upon my knightly feet, my sturdy calves flexing beneath their smart crested greaves, a poleyn hingeing on each noble knee with the silent slickness that only goose grease can confer, and a bright cuisse flashing on each sinewy thigh; while, downstairs, my loyal squire sat devotedly buffing tasset and pauldron and vambrace, and anything else he could identify from his master's trusty thesaurus.

Or possibly not. The sixth-century class structure being, as I understand it, a tad less flexible than today's, the odds are minimal that King Arthur would have fancied me for knighthood and derring-do: the closest I should have come to any Round Table tuck-in would have been circling it with my forelock in one hand and the pudding platter in the other, and God help me if a blob of custard fell on Launcelot's coulter. Or perhaps, given my present trade, somersaulting in the grate with titchy brass bells tinkling on my hat, and telling my yawning liege lords the one about the Roman, the Dane, and the Jute.

However, they have not twigged this in Charleston, South Carolina. Not only do they not realise I am not a gentleman, they firmly believe I am up for knighthood. The they concerned are the Chevaliers de la Table Ronde, and they have just written to me – on something impressively vellumoid – to say that, after long deliberation, I have been selected as a fit candidate for ennoblement to their distinguished ranks. They do not say how they came to do this deliberating, but my guess is that since, down the long arches of the years, I have somehow managed to have been made both an Honorary Colonel in the Confederate Army and an Ensign of the Tennessee Volunteers Overseas, I have somehow, willy-nilly, wormed my way – perhaps, quite literally, as some kind of virus – on to a Dixieland computer network pledged to embarrassing Europeans of a liberal bent. It is not beyond credibility, either, that one or other of the Bush family has had a sly hand in all this.

But what is more interesting than the Chevalier's provenance is their declared motive. They are, they tell me, pledged to the return of chivalry. Nothing new there: the dream of courtoisie persists, else man would not have so regularly given it a revitalising kick, fleeing into its beguiling arms whenever the prevailing reality grew grisly – Spenser turning to Fairielande from the mire of the Elizabethan court, Tennyson preferring idyllic Avalon to the mundane practicality of signal box and water closet, and Hollywood running away from virtually everything towards virtual Sherwoods and Camelots. Given this, you might reasonably guess that what the Charleston Chevaliers – a trifle unsettlingly, my mind's eye sees them all in sequined flapper drag, with bobbed hair and bee-sting mouths, dancing frenetically to Bix Beiderbecke's cornet, but I'll get over it – want to get away from is the miasma of Iraq, but that is not the case. What they want to get away from, quite patently, is the ever-worsening threat to all they hold dear (as it were) from feminism. I know this from their enclosed roster meticulously detailing precisely what I have to commit myself to if I wish to pass the test for knighthood.

In broad, I have to miss no opportunity 'to make ladies feel like ladies.' In narrow, this means I have not merely to tip my hat, open doors, pull back chairs, tote dat bag, lif dat tray, push dat trolley, squeeze dat gas-pump, and light dat fag, and of course manfully refuse any lady her offer to pick up a restaurant tab or bar check. I have also to commit myself, at all times, to telling women what pretty little things they are, what a really great job they are doing for us menfolk, and, get this, Germaine, 'striving always to persuade them – especially those, and they are many, who appear to you to be obsessed with their so-called careers – that marriage and motherhood should be the highest aspiration of every woman in the world.'

Well, Chevaliers, thanks, you do me great honour, but I fear I am not the timber of which true knights are made. I lack the right stuff. Faced with one of your modern dragons, I would chicken out. I just couldn't do the derring.

One Flu Over The Chicken's Nest

THERE is a chicken out there with my name on it. I do not know what the chicken's own name is, I do not even know where the there is, I know only that in the course of a long life's wondering about what might one day nip that life in the bud, I had never, until now, reckoned it would be a chicken.

Because the chicken had always been man's best friend. This was admittedly something of a one-way street, since in order to demonstrate her friendship the chicken had first to give up her babies for scrambling, then herself to be throttled, plucked, drawn, quartered, roasted, and eaten, finally submitting to the friendliest gesture of all: getting her sucked-clean furcula snapped in half to grant the luckier of her last two friends a wish. As if that were not enough, the loving bond between man and bird continued beyond the grave: man, praying that mortality might not be the end, looked at his dear departed's bones, took stock, and the chicken came back as soup.

But all that is over, now. The worm has turned; and though we may all be shaken that it has suddenly turned so utterly, it's pretty clear that it was the absence of turned worms that started it. For once man had worked out that he might benefit even more from the friendship by depriving the chicken not only of wriggling organic tucker but also of fresh air, sunlight and free range sex, and banging her up in concentration camps to be force fed on a broad range of industrial delicacies to both stimulate her growth and circumscribe her lust, the worm that turned was unstoppably bound to relocate itself. It became the worm in the bud that is about to be nipped.

Because they come home to roost, chickens. The one with my name on it might be doing so right now, since though it is sunrise here in the West, it is sunset there in the East, and she may well turn in early because she has this cough, she has this headache, she has this runny beak; probably only a cold, cry the others, there's a lot of it about, but they are just clucking to keep their spirits up, they know sure as eggs is eggs that one of their best friends is going to show up any moment now to strangle them all and chuck them on the bonfire. But what if the worm in the bud is a new mutant strain, and the best friend himself feels a bit under the weather tomorrow? Nothing to worry about, says his wife, putting a caring hand to his thumping brow; but she works on the desk at Chen Ding Airport and next day the hand is passing a ticket to a happy fellow winging back to Manchester with a nice new contract for this or that, jostling the Ringway crowds as he hurries home to . . .

Then again, that may not be the chicken with my name on it: mine may be much closer to home, because it is no longer a chicken at all but a tasty nugget of mechanically recovered slurry bulked up with polyphosphates and cosmetically reconstituted reptile organs from more than one country of origin, pullulating, inside its fetching mahogany scab, with enough hormones to sprout jordans on a priapic rat, and sloshing about in a zesty sauce made to a secret recipe discovered on Josef Mengele's Rolodex. Anyone tucking in to a £1.99 jumbo bucket of this muck deserves all he gets, of course, but none of us is safe: I have walked past my local Colonel Bogey and felt my nostrils clog with bacterial pong. I could keel over any minute.

And if I did, well-wishers would be advised to take great care where they laid me: for were the inhalation not to see me off, the pillow beneath my head might. For, as you'll have read, the industrial use of feathers is to be much more rigorously regulated, because unscrupulous merchants and stuffers have been cutting expensive goose down and duck down with cheap chicken down, off which anything could be caught – probably through the ear, personally one of my least favourite sites for catchable items, since they could be down that hole quicker than the White Rabbit and, once out of sight, up to God knows what.

So, then, is there anything we can do to lengthen the odds against our being felled, one way or another, by what has clearly become man's worst enemy? Yes, just possibly, through alternative therapy – the alternative to lurching into a hospital where the kitchens cook the chicken which any day now will be revealed to be the source of all NHS cross-infection, i.e. nobody's fault – because laughter, University of Maryland boffins declared last week, is the best medicine. If you feel anything nasty coming on, a good joke, their research shows, sets the immune system up a treat.

Provided, of course, it doesn't involve a chicken crossing a road.

Time Out

THE worst thing about being a child of the twentieth century is that you end up an adult of the twenty-first. The present is a foreign country; they do things differently here.

It is time to talk about time. I do not know what time it is, because my watch isn't working. You will say, hang on, you could look out of the window, you live next door to a church with a clock, but what you do not know is that the church clock isn't working, either. Once upon a time, a man with a green baize apron and a bag of spanners would have pedalled up on a squeaky Rudge, leaned it against the railings, and climbed up to sort things out. But the vicar cannot get a man with a green baize apron, these days, for love nor money; since, when it comes to churches, both are now in short supply.

Hang further on, you will say, we know you write on a computer, why don't you just look at the top of the screen where it says the time is 11.06 p.m.? Because the time is not 11.06 p.m. If it were, the sun wouldn't be out. Now, while there is probably a way of adjusting a computer clock, I do not know what it is, because computers do not come with manuals any more, the way they did in the twentieth century, having become so complicated that a manual would be bigger and pricier than the computer. I could fiddle with the keyboard in the hope of getting lucky and finding how you adjust the clock, but whenever I have fiddled with the keyboard, I have never got lucky, I have only got unlucky, and been forced to take the computer back to where I bought it, usually in the middle of an article which has vanished for good.

Writing didn't used to be like that when I was a child of the twentieth century. It is nearly 50 years since I first wrote for money, and I wrote for it with a pencil and paper, which I could carry around in my trouser pocket and use anywhere. The pencil and paper never went wrong, unless you count a bit of sharpening, but there was always room in my trouser pocket for a penknife, too. I cannot get my computer into my trouser pocket, and it goes wrong all the time, but editors and publishers do not accept paper any more, and anyway, I have lost the longhand knack.

It is also nearly 50 years since I had a watch that didn't go wrong. My dad bought it for me when, at 12, I first went off to Scout camp, because he was a caring man and knew that when the Scoutmaster shouted: 'Synchronise watches!' his son would look a prat without something to synchronise. It was a terrific watch: not only could you wind it up every night and discover it was still telling the right time the next morning; during that night, in the tent, you could read by it. It was the world's most luminous watch, because little was known about radioactivity. If Hans Blix had found a watch like that on Saddam Hussein's bedside table, George W. wouldn't be in the embarrassing situation he is in today. All in all, I was probably lucky to have it pinched four years later: the thief's grandchildren may well have two heads by now.

But it kept perfect time, and never went wrong; unlike the one I replaced it with, using the first money I ever earned with pencil and paper. This was described as an automatic, because you didn't have to wind it, all you had to do was shake your wrist every half an hour to stop it stopping. It did not, however, stop people asking what was wrong with your wrist, unless they were the sensitive kind who reckoned that an adolescent with an incurable tic might prefer not to have attention constantly drawn to it. After a few years, I got sick of all the shaking, especially as my left forearm was growing stronger than my right – which may explain why my tennis is so lousy – so I got married to allow my new father-in-law to buy me a Bulova Accutron as a wedding present. It was the first electronic watch, run on a battery which powered a tuning-fork. The first person to ask me: 'What's that peculiar humming noise?' was Mrs Coren. On our wedding-night.

I had a lot of electric watches after that, always two simultaneously, because when one was sent away for a new battery, it didn't come back for a month, with a bill to include service, new crystal, new waterproofing, and a lot of other stuff to enable three figures to be aggregated. That is why I was so happy, last year, to find the world's first sun-powered watch: no winding, no battery, just be sure your wrist is regularly exposed to light.

Oh yes, and keep it away from all static electricity sources. They didn't tell me that when I bought it. They told me yesterday when I rang up to ask why it was on the fritz. 'Do you wear it,' they asked, 'when using a computer?'

Stands England Where It Did?

BOOKS were always important in my family: I grew up surrounded by them. My mother's father ran one, her brother ran one, and her cousin ran one. Not licensed, mind: they were off-course bookies, in an era when, of course, the trade was illicit. You could go down for it. And I did: I went down to The Dog and Duck, and I stood outside, waiting for men who were old enough to sit inside to come outside and pass me their betting slips, so that I could slip down to this relative or that and slip them the slips and the legal tender that illegally went with them. I was a runner; and not, at 12, a bad one – when, perhaps because of this early training, I became an even better one, I could be found running round the Iffley Road track after Jeffrey Archer, possibly the iffiest couple ever to do so: that the entire Thames Valley constabulary wasn't running after us is down only to history's poor sense of timing.

So, then, the three themes laid out on today's wonky stall are gambling, pubs, and Oxford, and I am flogging them as a package: what is up for grabs is nothing less than Olde Englande, and I rather fear that when Newe Laboure has finished grabbing it, there will be a whole lot less.

Half a century ago, Britain's gambling culture was a bit special: it was remarkably animated, relying not only on runners, but on duckers and divers, and bobbers and weavers. If you wanted to bet on horses or dogs, the only legitimate way was to go to the track, but if you wanted to bet on them anywhere else, or on anything else, there was no legitimate way at all. You had to descend quite literally into an underworld of basement spielers, where dodgy entrepreneurs had paid off dodgier coppers to turn a blind eye while cards were riffled and wheels spun and dice tossed, and wads of cash slid from hand to hand, usually in one direction only.

It wasn't an evil world, just a bit naughty, a bit wicked, a bit, well, gamey – and very hard to find. It didn't get evil until gambling was legitimised, when it became very easy to find: it may always have been a mug's game, but now everyone, effortlessly, could be a mug. Worse yet, it all grew, though I lack the space to explain in detail how, less British; and now, under the crackpot croupiership of New Labour, it is about to become not British at all. It is to be Las Vegan.

The pub isn't going to be Las Vegan, though: it is going to be continental. I'm not entirely certain what the Prime Minister thinks he means by that – does he envisage us sitting around toasting Derrida in pastis to the sound of accordions, does he expect us to link arms and chorus our ambitions for the Sudetenland, are we to slump beside our umpteenth vodka, weeping for our dead babushka, or, having sluiced down our ploughman's taramasalata with our umpteenth ouzo, smash the plate? – but whatever he thinks he wants from 24-hour drinking, what he is not going to get is 'Time, gentlemen, please!' as the tea-towels drop over the pumps while the last ha'penny is shoved, and softly belching grown-ups toddle out into the earlyish night, less plastered than is required for vomiting into a letter-box before chucking a gravel bin through Dixon's window and butting an OAP.

You will, I imagine, have spotted that I am not merely wailing objectively on behalf of all the babies whose own drowning cries cannot be heard over the Government's disappearing bathwater: and since you have detected just a smidgeon of value judgment in today's farrago, you will not be surprised to learn where I stand on the news that, because of the Government's annual underfunding of £100m, Oxford University is to cut the number of British undergraduates it admits and 'vigorously recruit' more foreign students, who pay the full whack for their degrees.

Yes, where I stand is four-square behind the Department of Education, punching the air; because its stinginess will ensure that Oxford does *not* go down the cultural drain. Filling the place with foreigners is the surest way of preserving it: walk down any Oxford street, and the flannelled fool pedalling towards you on an old Rudge bicycle with an oar on one gowned shoulder, a teddy bear on the other, and a copy of *Zuleika Dobson* tucked under the leather-elbowed arm of his college-badged blazer is bound to be from either Minneapolis or Tokyo; where he has always dreamed of dreaming spires.

And now he is cycling to the Bodleian Library, to find out what a crumpet is, and how to prong it.

All The World's A Stage

CULTURE stalwarts have been plunged into gloom at the news that many London theatres are about to go, literally, dark, after an unprecedented loss of audiences; and since the Society of London Theatre is at a loss to understand the loss, let me explain it.

For the fact is that, while it will be agreed that a night at a great London theatre is a wonderfully enriching experience, more and more people are discovering that, with a little effort, they can replicate that experience without actually coughing up £40 a head. Mrs Coren and I certainly have.

It is Friday night. After an enervating week, we feel we owe ourselves the tonic treat of *The West Wing, Friends,* and *The Simpsons*. Like the theatre, it starts at 7.45, too early to eat before, so we shall eat after. We leave the house in good time, and park as far away as possible, allowing us to arrive back at the house, breathless and rainsoaked, just in time to take our seats. My chair, such is the fortuitous construction of our living-room, has been placed behind a pillar; Mrs Coren's chair is behind mine. In order to see either half of the screen, I have to lean first to the left, then to the right, as of course does Mrs Coren, alternatively. From time to time she will strike me on the shoulder and remind me that some people have come here to see the telly. I whip round and tell her that if that's the case, she should stop repeating the actor's lines, because it prevents me from hearing the next ones. She retaliates by opening a two kilo box of Maltesers.

At the end of *The West Wing*, rush to the lavatory, only to find she has beaten me to it. I queue. By the time I get back, *Friends* has started, and she won't let me take my seat. I have to stand at the back, whence the screen is so small, it could be ping-pong from Beijing. At the commercial break, Mrs Coren runs out into the downpouring street to smoke a fag, but the break is brief; this time, I make her stand at the back. But I do not enjoy the second half, for I have fetched myself an ice cream, and the little spoon has broken off in the tub and flicked raspberry ripple onto my trousers. I move about so much in trying to rub it off that Mrs Coren calls the manager. Since it is my turn to be the manager, I tell myself to sit still or leave.

Before *The Simpsons* starts, there is time for a gin and tonic. Or would be, if the woman in front of me weren't ordering a brown sherry, a Guinness, a dry martini, a San Pellegrino, three packets of low-calorie pork scratchings, and can she have a tray? When I get back, ginless, the woman is sitting in my seat. I do not make a fuss, because it is her turn to be the manager, and she will throw me out.

At the end of *The Simpsons*, we go to the hall cupboard to get our coats, but they have vanished, and by the time we get downstairs to the kitchen, it is too late for a hot dinner. Mrs Coren asks me if I can run to a sandwich, but I tell her (in Polish) that the cook has gone home, and I am not allowed, under the terms of my temporary visa, to prepare food. So we go out into what is now sleet to collect the car, which has, of course, been (a) clamped, (b) towed, or/and (c) trashed. Luckily, there are no cabs and the last bus has gone, allowing us to walk home shouting at one another. It has been a magical evening. It has been what theatre is all about.

Marching On My Stomach

I was much moved at our great Prime Minister's personal intervention in the furore over unsatisfactory school dinners: not only did it stand in a great British tradition, it took me back . . .

Deer Mr Cherchill:
Yesday we had Rusian sallad again. It was the thurd time this weak. The thing with Rusian sallad is it looks like sombody

else has alredy et it. Nobody on mi tabel tuched it, not even Gerald Bottley, who eets wurms. We all want to fite for you wen we gro up, but if we do not eet, we will not gro up at all, our feet wil not reech tank pedals, we will be too week to pul triggars, wen we jump out on parashoots we will be too lite and get blone all over the plase. You will hav to do somthing. PS, wel done at Allermane, pleese congrachlate all conserned, yores A. Coren, 4b.

Dear Master Coren:
Russian salad is very good for you. That is why your Uncle Joe is enjoying such formidable success at Stalingrad, where, subsisting as they do entirely on sauerkraut, the enfeebled Narzis (sic) are about to be annihilated. My advice to you is to eat with your eyes shut, and make believe: you must say to 4b, 'Let us therefore brace ourselves to our dinner and so stuff ourselves that if the British Commonwealth and its Empire last for a thousand years, men will still say 'That was the finest steak.' Yours etc, WC

Dear Mr Cherchill:
Thank you for yore lettar. We dint half larf, do they reely call you WC, it must get on yore nurves, they call me Acorn, it is not too bad, Gerald Bottley is call Bummole, and I wunt like to tell you about Brian Cunliffe. I am not suprised the Narzis are sic, we had sourkrout yesday, even with yore eyes shut it was like string in vinniger. Why can't we ever hav meat? They give us this sort of red lino and they say it is prest beef, but they are Hers, posibly Germen spies with orders to kill us by choaking. Good werk in Casablanca, by the way, did Mr Roosevelt give you eny chewing-gumm? Wot we wuld reely like is some chicken. Culd you fix that? For yore infmation, I am not the master. Our Master is Old Farty. Yores A. Coren (boy)

Dear Master Coren:
Some chicken? I must say, you have some neck: none of us will have chicken until Hitler is defeated, upon which joyous day we shall eat it on the beaches, we shall eat it on the landing grounds, we shall eat it in the fields and in the streets, we shall eat it in the hills, we shall never stop eating it; but for the present, I must urge you to persevere with the pressed beef of old England. I also advise you to do the same with your studies: I cannot but observe that you are presently writing the sort of English up with which I will not put.
Yours etc, Churchill

Dear Cherchill:
It is not my fawlt my riting is rottan, it is on acount of my diet. If yu do not get propper food yu canot constrate, also bad behaviar, we do not play hoo can widdel ferthest up the jim wall becos we want to, we do not flik blodge bullits or speke wen we are not spoke to or shuv 4a's heds down bogs becos we like it, we cannot help ourselves due to eeting rubish. Eg, yesday we had frogsporn, and no, befor yu say it, not tapioca, Bummole had a reel tadpoal in his, he sed wot the fuk is this, and Old Farty clowted him. By the way, wot is soft underbelly? I saw yu menshunned it in Old Farty's newspaper when he rolled it up as a weppon for Bummole's hed. My mum says yu get it on pork, but yu hav to sleep with the butcher. I am at a loss to understand, probly due to diet againe. Well dun about D-Day, tho.
Yours, A. Coren

Dear Coren:
Thank you. Yes, the war is indeed advancing rather well, and thus it may well be that this great island race will soon

be facing a general election. I wonder, as a reward for her exemplary moral integrity, would your dear mother accept my personal gift of a nice York ham? I am also taking the liberty of instructing your school to put extra sultanas in the spotted dick. With more custard. This is not the end. It is not even the beginning of the end. But it is, perhaps, the end of the beginning.
Most sincerely, Winston

Private Lives

YOU will have seen at the weekend that a Yates's Wine Lodge in Nottingham, deeply concerned about the grim consequences of binge-drinking – riots, fights, vandalism, breakages, raids, and the myriad other appalling anti-social manifestations which, unchecked, can seriously threaten the profits of binge-drinking – and finding its own bouncers unequal to the Cerberean task, has hit on the idea of paying members of the Nottinghamshire Constabulary to police their premises on a private basis.

Not surprisingly, especially in a city whose law so recently had its knuckles rapped for being on the ends of unacceptably short arms, a public furore has followed. Among the outraged civic clamour, however, you will not hear my voice, but this has nothing to do with my living miles from the Nottingham earshot; what it has everything to do with is my conviction that it is time this benighted country introduced a system by which rich people in need of law and order could go privately.

Because it is self-evident that the more property you have, the more you will lose to villains eager to nick it off you; ergo, the broader should be your rights when endeavouring to thwart them. It is preposterous that a multimillionaire whose drum has just been turned over should have to stand in line for a 999 visit, a CID investigation, the minimal chance of an arrest and the remoter one of a conviction, as if he were of no more significance than some decrepit old biddy who had been mugged for her derisorily titchy pension.

More even than this, the well-heeled should not have to wait for the crime to be committed to enjoy the full protection the bank-balance allows: they should be able to ring a special number whenever, say, they intend visiting a cashpoint, or walking to the pillar-box with an important letter, or going out for the evening wearing a diamond choker/platinum Rolex/other fine bling, and having to park the Bentley in some dark alley; at the call, two senior and fully tooled-up policemen would arrive immediately, one to accompany them, and the other to squat in their vacated premises.

You will say, hang on, the rich can already hire private security men to do this, but that is not the same thing at all: partly because private security men are not empowered to arrest, partly because they cannot even adequately confront, given that they are not permitted to carry weapons, but mainly because most of them have either recently come out of Parkhurst themselves, or know a gang who have. Nor would they be any use if a rich man's cat went missing, or the people next door were pledging their troth too noisily, or there was something about the relief milkman which struck the rich man as iffy. If any such cloud were to appear on the rich man's horizon, he should be able to ring Scotland Yard, bark a credit card number, and be moved instantly to the head of the Pending Inquiries waiting-list.

I would go further: even when an arrest is made, it is often the case these days that an inept judge, flash lawyers, inexpert witnesses, and a thick jury will let the criminal off, accepting his defence that he found your Modigliani in a skip, or was simply performing a generous deed because your wife's tiara appeared to be uncomfortably entangled in her hair. Clearly, this outcome is totally unacceptable: if you are in the fortunate position of being able to afford it, you should be allowed to hire your own private judge and jury, so that the man your own private policeman has arrested will be found guilty as charged, manacled as painfully as possible, and sent down for the term you have specified on your order form. Or, in really irritating cases, hanged by you personally: since there is no capital punishment, you would not of course be allowed to hang him by the neck until he was dead, but he could dangle for a bit, certainly until it put the roses in his cheeks.

I realise that woolly liberals among you may argue that there should not be one law for the rich and another for the poor, but I think they are forgetting one little word: insurance. We are fortunate to live in a culture that with each passing day encourages more and more people to make provision for themselves, and I find it hard to believe that some benevolent company – let us, for argument's sake, call it Direct Crime – would not, if my suggestions were adopted, spring selflessly to the nation's aid.

Mad About The Boy

THIS morning, something dunked onto the doormat which dropped my jaw so far that the rest of me was catapulted back twenty-odd years to a year made odder than all the rest by an incident itself so odd that, even now, the memory of it, as I type, sends hot droplets coursing down my forehead into my eyes, blurring the words' arrival on the screen.

At that time, I was Editor of *Punch*, and my little cadre of wags and I were cobbling together a parody of *The Times*'s great stablemate, some would say unstablemate, the *Sun*. This of course required us to come up with a Page Three Stunna consonant with the spirit of the enterprise, and after some roisterous ferreting around in the dusty stacks of the Keystone Press Agency, we eventually found, among its ten million photographs, a figure that might have given the stacks their name.

Nor was Miranda just a shape which, chronology permitting, would have put Jordan in the shade – certainly if Miss Price were sitting at Miranda's feet with the sun behind them – but also a face: from beneath a demonstrably undeserved halo of platinum hair, cornflower eyes twinkled lasciviously above a pouting moue glossed to the size and lusciousness of a glazed doughnut. More yet: there was something else about Miranda which outflanked even all this desirability, and made it, for our purposes, utterly irresistable. Within seconds, we had whisked the snapshot across Fleet Street into our editorial bunker, gummed it to our layout, and, cackling, sped it to the printers.

Some two weeks later, I received a Telex from the captain of a destroyer bobbing in the Persian Gulf. I shall name neither him nor his ship, given that it may well have been bobbing more than standing orders required, thanks to the fact that the crew had recently received their copy of *Punch,* and fallen head over heels (this being how it is with hammocks), for Miranda. One copy, however, was not enough: could I, the skipper begged, send a further few dozen, for pinning up, which he would personally subsidise?

Well done, I hear you cry: not only did you pull off both an editorial and a commercial coup, you did your bit for the serving man. You made Jolly Jack Tar a little jollier. At a stroke. You cry this because you do not know, just as the crew of HMS *Nameless* did not know, what I knew – that Miranda was a bloke. Miranda was a drag queen: this was the something else which had tickled our callow editorial fancy. So I didn't reply to the Telex. How could I? I dared neither reveal the truth, nor supply further copies of the lie (though one or two of my staff suggested I do both, on the grounds that not all the sailors love a nice girl). Instead, I tried to forget about it; and succeeded. Until just now, when onto the mat fell the thing that jogged the memory.

It was a book: *Howard Hughes: Hell's Angel,* by Darwin Porter, about which the publisher wants me to say something nice. Not easy. For, as I flipped its pages, I spotted the name of Clark Gable, and stayed the thumb: had he, I wondered, been in one of Hughes's films? No: he had been in one of Hughes's beds. Not content, as many would have been, with Ginger Rogers, Katharine Hepburn, Ava Gardner, and all the rest, Howard had pulled Clark.

I cannot be alone in thinking Ms Porter has done the world something of a disservice. Oh, sure, we are all men of that world, and, no less to the point, women of it, too, and have taken on board the twinnings of Laurence Olivier and Danny Kaye, or even, albeit with perhaps a slightly sharper gasp, Errol Flynn and Randolph Scott; but Clark Gable, seminal benchmark of so many hitherto immortally romantic films? Shall any of us ever again be able to watch Rhett Butler hurtling up that staircase without – even if for only a nanosecond – imagining not Vivien Leigh panting in his manly arms, but the barmy old aviator, while the great four-poster above awaits the passionate commingling of their two moustaches?

Tread softly, because you tread on my dreams. I give not a fig for their private lives, but their public lives are mine. Who, after this, can begin to guess what other couplings lurk in what other woodsheds, trembling at the footfall of a coffin-chaser with a trick to turn? Jimmy Cagney and Spencer Tracy, perhaps? Lee Marvin and Karl Maiden? Yes, you are not wrong, it is a dinner-party game, now, and we shall never be free of it.

Still, it has at least, and at last, freed me of one ancient burden. I know now that I was right, all those years ago, not to write to HMS *Nameless* and set her, as it were, straight.

Me and My Shadow

As a colonel in the Confederate Air Force and the proud father of a pelican, I spent a somewhat fraught Bank Holiday Monday. It would, mind, have been even more fraught had the banks not been on holiday: the constant terror that a man in full dress uniform might at any minute turn up at a branch of Lloyds TSB, one hand holding a pelican's leash and the other withdrawing all the money advanced for a book I haven't yet written, would have distracted me from the work in hand, with unfathomable consequences. I was also fortunate that the work in hand had prevented me from joining the holiday jams lurching towards coast and garden centre: had I done that, I might well have returned to find my house owner-occupied by a family from Nuneaton, possibly Tring, whose Doberman – since they hadn't had time to change the locks – would, as I stepped into the hall, have eaten my arm.

Do you have, as Rolf Harris might put it, any inkling yet of what that work in hand is? I say Rolf Harris, but who knows, he could be any bearded joker with three legs and a wet palette currently whooping it up in Acapulco on purloined didgeridoo royalties, having had his original committed to a bin on the signature of three psychiatrists who had never signed any such thing.

Yes, you have it now: the issue is identity-theft, and the work in hand was shredding. I had held off buying a shredder for some time, partly because I didn't want to acknowledge that I now inhabited a world in which it had become necessary, partly because I didn't want to lose any fingers, but I finally succumbed last week to the incessant television hectoring by Alistair McGowan that if anything ended up in my dustbin but grass-cuttings, then hundreds of globally-strewn cyberclones would soon be driving Ferraris and gargling Petrus and bedding celebrity ladyboys until the bailiffs stove my door in to distrain upon everything I owned and, discovering I no longer owned it, bunged me into Belmarsh.

Monday started off prudently enough, bank statements, utilities bills, VAT-bumf, council tax demands, credit-card counterfoils and all the other dull bourgeois detritus humming into chaff through the chomping blades, but after it had gone, I realised I had barely started. There was so much of me left on paper: I could front up for the Lord's Test only to find myself barred from the pavilion for impersonating me, I could be told by the chemist that my prescription had already been filled and I should henceforth have to stay the Reaper with bladderwort and joss, my car could wind up ferrying Armalites through the Bogside until Special Branch megaphones hove to outside my house informing me that I had three minutes to come out with my hands up, and if I did not shred the cherished adoption certificate, some base Tichborne claimant might appear at the London Zoo and tell my pelican that he was its real father. They're gullible birds. As for my Confederate Air Force colonelcy, bestowed in 1987 for wag services rendered in Atlanta, if the accreditation fell into the wrong hands and my doppelganger got up in a plane and fired on Fort Sumter, I would be blamed for starting Civil War Two. Being made, as the result, a colonel in Al Qaida would be scant consolation.

Trickier yet, as I shredded I listened to my radio – if it is my radio, it may well be licensed to a Mallorcan by now – and therefore to a lot of hysterical gargle about the French referendum. Since one of the constituents of the exconstitution, I gather, was the eurowide strengthening of privacy protection, the landmark *Non* may well act as a carte blanche for the hitherto hesitant. What, for example, is to stop a Pole from poaching my membership of the P. G. Wodehouse Society, spending a week at the Paris Ritz in spats and a monocle as Gussie Fink-Nottleski, and charging the whole thing to my account? And God knows how many points are, as I write, being totted up on my driving licence by Maltese joy-riders.

Indeed, it has just occurred to me that you may not be reading what I'm writing at all, unless you are an Eskimo, given that it is being hacked out on a computer prior to e-mailing and therefore highly vulnerable to turning up in tomorrow's *Inuit Morning Advertiser*, since the shredder and I were unable to find the Post-It on which I scribbled my password in 1997. Some years back, it either blew off the printer when the daily opened a window to let the smoke out, or someone nicked it. I hadn't thought about it, until now.

Nor had I thought about ID cards. These will be dropping onto our mats any minute, once we have collectively forked out 18 billion pounds, and I shall snatch mine up immediately. No time must be lost in shredding it.

Losing Your Bottle

IT being humid this morning and my attic window open, I can hear – though he is buried far away – my grandfather turning in his grave.

Not so odd, you reply, we live in plummeting times, there is much to spin Britain's buried grandpas: were you to stroll through Stoke Poges churchyard today, the lowing of the winding herd would be drowned by the racket of grumpy dead men. You have a point – but not this one: for my grandfather took life as it came (took it, indeed, as it went) without complaint at its decline. You would not have caught him staring glumly out of his Wembley window and observing that it is not now as it hath been of yore.

Even in 1943. Or, rather, especially in 1943. Because my grandfather knew not only what he was fighting for, but also that his country was as equal to that fight as she had ever been. I say fighting, but since he was the exact age I am now, he was armed only with an ARP warden's helmet and a stirrup pump; he knew, in short, what he was fire-watching for. You could tell that from the helmet: black (so that the Luftwaffe wouldn't spot his moonlit silver hair), it had two brief messages daubed on it in white. One read 'Dig here for Dave!', the other 'God save the King!' In the event of his being buried by rubble, my grandfather wanted the world to know both who had died with his gumboots on, and what he had died for.

But the world wouldn't need to be told that, if, like me, it had shared his breakfast every day. When he came in from his night's watching, his plate would be ready in front of him, and in front of it would be three bottles: HP brown sauce, Lea & Perrins' Worcester sauce, and Camp coffee; but the bottle which wasn't there was as telling as those which were. His ritual was unvaried: I would sit opposite him, jaws glued together by my grandmother's porridge, and he would tap the bottles with his eggy knife and remind me that all were supplied by appointment to His Majesty King George VI. More yet, he would bang on, HP sauce was named for the Houses of Parliament: you can see that from the picture of Big Ben on the label. So not only our gracious King and Queen, he would explain, were smacking the bottom of their sauce bottles at the exact same moment as their loyal subjects, so were all our great, and democratically elected, leaders. God knows what bloody Hitler and bloody Tojo are sloshing on their breakfasts this morning, was his invariable coda, but you can be bloody sure it isn't this.

Don't swear, my grandmother would say, he's only five, but he would ignore her, because there was one more very important point he was already making about HP sauce: it had been invented in 1899, at the start of the Boer War, so that the soldiers of the queen would have something to help bully beef go down. And if you want to know what a soldier of the queen looked like, he would add – not without a justified grin at his polyglot segue – have a shufti at the coffee. I did not have to ask what a shufti was: he had explained it on umpteen similar occasions when passing me the Camp coffee bottle, because the label showed a kilted Indian Army subaltern being served a silver-plattered cup by an egregiously devoted Sikh batman.

That my grandfather saw British history in exclusively gustatory terms would finally be confirmed with the splash of Lea & Perrins onto the bread he used to wipe his plate: he would observe, yet again, that the bloody Yanks could not pronounce Worcester. He was no fan of the Americans: he had waited three grisly years for them to join him in the Flanders mud, and well-nigh as long this time around; and therein lies the significance of the bottle that wasn't there. He wouldn't have Heinz ketchup in the house. Not only was it American, the American who invented it, in 1885, had been born German. That my grandfather never pointed out that 1885 was the year Gordon was killed at Khartoum, where were the bloody Yanks that time, need you bloody ask, has often, down the long arches of the years, puzzled me.

Reader, you've been very patient: you have waited so long, without once interrupting me to ask why my grandfather is turning in his grave today. He is doing it because today it was announced that Heinz was taking over both HP and Lea & Perrins. Even as I write, I hear his voice cursing the fact that, henceforth, Worcester is forever doomed to have three bloody syllables.